The Business of Banking

Fourth Edition

Geoffrey Lipscombe
and
Keith Pond

The Chartered Institute of Bankers

Financial World Publishing
c/o The Chartered Institute of Bankers
IFS House
4-9 Burgate Lane
Canterbury
Kent
CT1 2XJ
United Kingdom

Telephone: 01227 812012
e-mail: editorial@ifslearning.com

Financial World Publishing publications are published by The Chartered Institute of Bankers, a non-profit making registered educational charity.
The Chartered Institute of Bankers believes that the sources of information upon which the book is based are reliable and has made every effort to ensure the complete accuracy of the text. However, neither CIB, the author nor any contributor can accept any legal responsibility whatsoever for consequences that may arise from errors or omissions or any opinion or advice given.

Typeset by John Smith

Printed by Antony Rowe Ltd

© The Chartered Institute of Bankers 2002

ISBN 0-85297-671-2

CONTENTS

1   What is banking all about?   1

2   Money   13

3   More about money   31

4   The recent history of banking and finance   51

5   Banks, building societies and insurance companies   69

6   The City of London and the Bank of England   89

7   The banker-customer relationship   105

8   Customers and accounts   125

9   Payment methods   149

10 Funds transfer: cheques and the clearing systems   171

11 The collecting bank and the paying bank   191

12 Elementary lending   209

13 Elementary security for lending   223

14 Bankers and insolvency   241

    Glossary   255

    Index   267

Preface

This book was originally written as a basic text for the Chartered Institute of Bankers' Banking Certificate paper 'The Business of Banking'. The book is a wide-ranging introduction to the position of retail banks, in particular, in the UK financial system.

In 1995 the text was updated and adopted at Loughborough University as a basic text on its 'Introduction to Banking' module, part of its well-known Banking & Finance degree.

Updated and republished in 1999 the book became popular in the UK and overseas. The current edition further updates and extends the text to incorporate major changes to the regulatory, economic, professional, commercial, technological and practical environments in which retail banks operate.

Readers will note that the valuable and up-to-date description of financial institutions, systems and markets alongside an introduction to payments systems, lending and the law relating to banking provide an excellent introduction to the UK banking scene.

The text is intended as a primer, an introduction to the wide and complex world of banking, and particular attention is drawn to the 'Further reading' sections at the end of each chapter. The texts cited are widely available and often provide more detailed coverage, or specific examples, of the topics in the chapters themselves.

Retail banks have undergone considerable changes in the last ten years, their capacity to react to economic, environmental, political, social and technological pressures will guarantee further changes in the decade to come. This book provides an excellent review of the business of banking today.

Thanks are due to Mrs Joyce Tuson at Loughborough University for her work in preparing the manuscript for publication.

Geoffrey Lipscombe and Keith Pond
Croydon and Loughborough
January 2002

About the Authors

Geoffrey Lipscombe BSc (Econ) FCIB is a former Economic Adviser to Lloyds Bank and is the Chartered Institute of Bankers' Chief Examiner for Economics and the Banks' Role in the Economy. He is editor of *The New Financial Review*, a publication aimed at teachers of A-level economics and formerly worked closely with the Banking Information Service.

Keith Pond BSc, ACIB, MPhil, MICM, ILTM is a former Manager with Midland Bank and was Midland Group Visiting Fellow at Loughborough University from 1986 to 1989. He is an Institute of Financial Services tutor, and Assignment writer and Chief Examiner for the Institute of Credit Management final stage paper Legal Proceedings and Insolvency. As a full-time lecturer in Banking and Economics at Loughborough University he has been involved in an EU project to establish a Banking Faculty in Kiev, Ukraine and has researched into Insolvency, Debt Counselling and Payments systems. Keith is a member of the Institute of Learning and Teaching in Higher Education.

1 What is it all about?

Objectives

After studying this chapter you should be able to:

☐ Describe the wide range of banking activities.

☐ State the various other subjects that a study of banking involves.

☐ Outline the developments in technology that have affected banking in the past and that will affect it even more in the future.

☐ Discuss the possible changes likely to affect the business of banking in the early years of the 21st century.

Introduction

'What is it all about?' Well, banking is about money. 'OK', you may answer, 'but accountancy is about money: so what is the difference between accountancy and banking?' You are right of course: accountancy is about money. But accountancy is concerned with recording and checking flows of money to and from a person or business and in planning to make a profit. Banking is different from accountancy because banks deal with the money itself when it is transferred from person to person, from business to business and from country to country. Banks also provide a home for people's money, which is something accountants do not do; and banks also lend money, which accountants certainly do not do.

There are three kinds of banking: retail banking, mortgage banking and wholesale banking.

1.   Retail banks are often known as High Street banks, because they have large branch networks, many of them comprising well over a thousand branches, usually located in the main shopping streets. Barclays, LloydsTSB, HSBC, National Westminster, Royal Bank of Scotland and Bank of Scotland are among the largest retail banks, with branches ranging from major ones in the City and the West End of London to small branches in West Country villages. The customers of retail banks range from enormous companies such as Shell, ICI, and BT to millions of people with their own personal accounts. Retail banks also run the clearing system, which will be explained later.

2.   Mortgage banks are those building societies which have chosen to become banks in the last ten years or so. Much of their business is mortgage lending rather than personal or commercial lending, although they are seeking to broaden their product range.

3.   Wholesale banks are found in the major financial centres of the world, eg London, New York, Frankfurt and Tokyo. They serve the major companies and have large-scale dealings with other banks throughout the world. They deal only in large amounts for large customers – £1 million or US$1 million is the usual minimum transaction. From these wholesale banks there have emerged investment banks engaged in buying and selling securities and foreign exchange, rather than accepting deposits and then lending these deposits.

The distinction between retail and wholesale banking is blurred because the largest retail banks also have important sections for wholesale banking.

Money

Money is the stock in trade of banks. But what is money?

When we were very young, money meant 'coins'. At primary school we probably learnt that money also came in notes, which were worth more than coins. Later we came across cheques, credit cards and cash dispensers.

Money can be defined as an asset, which is generally acceptable in payment for goods, services and for repaying debts. Everyday money comprises notes and coins but businesses and many individuals often prefer to use their balances with their banks and transfer these balances by cheques, as we shall see in Chapter 9.

Money is always changing its form. Animals were used as money centuries ago, then precious metals, then coins then notes, and then these 'bank deposits' (transferred by cheques). We are now moving towards some form of electronic money.

Whatever its exact form, money is important so we devote the next two chapters to it.

People

As in all life, people are important in business and banking – bank staff, managers and, most important, customers. And we must not forget the shareholders who own the banks and most of the businesses for which we may work. Dealing with people can be difficult and so a whole subject on management may be included in your studies.

One aspect of 'people management' is communication – written and oral. You should be able to write in such a way as to convince the readers of the correctness of the views you express without upsetting them too much and without leaving them unclear as to what you mean. You also need to be able to talk convincingly to people. Unfortunately, not all of us are equally endowed with these two skills – written and oral communication. Not even university teachers!

So far, in this section, we have regarded 'people' as individuals, but there is another way of analysing people – people in general, the general public, pressure groups etc. Since about 1980, banks have been heavily criticized by public opinion and the media, so certain changes have been made to improve relations. One of these was Good Banking, a voluntary code of practice drawn up by the banks, building societies and the organization that runs the clearings. We shall discuss the Banking Code (as it is now known) in greater detail later on in the book, and we shall quote the relevant sections.

The reason why we mention it here is to make the point that while personal relationships are highly important, so is the 'image' created by banks and other businesses in the minds of the general public.

Law

Law is the system of rules enforced by the courts governing our behaviour, especially disputes we have with other people. For bankers this comprises largely our relations with our customers but it also covers relations between the bank and its employees and, unfortunately, the ownership of money deposited with banks by terrorists and drug traffickers. This latter aspect is part of criminal law which includes such matters as fraud, stolen cheque cards and chequebooks and which is becoming of increasing concern to banks. However, most 'law relating to banking' is civil law.

Accountancy

Accountancy is concerned with money, but largely from an historical viewpoint. How much did a company or person spend? How much did it sell or receive in income? How much are a firm's stocks of finished goods and raw materials worth? Did it make a profit last year?

In the past 50 years or so, accountancy has also been used to help businesses to plan their future success, and firms of accountants have set up specialist 'management consultancy' sections to help their client companies to grow.

Taxation is also an important service offered by firms of

accountants, which prepare tax returns for wealthy individuals and businesses. Although most people can do very well without an accountant, every business needs one, if only to let the business-person get on with producing and selling while the accountant looks after the records.

Not surprisingly, accountancy may be an important part of your course.

Because banks are businesses, they need to use accounting principles in their day-to-day work, but they also use them in discussions with business customers. One very important banking activity is lending money and a bank must be certain that it is lending to financially healthy businesses or individuals and not to those that may collapse and leave the bank with its loan unpaid. Therefore, bankers must be able to understand accounts.

Lending

Anybody can lend money – it's getting the loan back that can be hard! So, banks employ specialist lending officials, often aided by computer programs, to take the decisions as to whether or not to lend and, if so, how much to lend. In this book we touch upon lending in a later chapter.

Lending can be a very profitable part of a bank's operations but it can be very risky, and poor lending has caused many banks to fail in previous centuries.

Economics

This is another subject often studied at greater length. At this stage, we can define economics as the 'science of prices'. When you realize that the price of your labour will be your salary, and that the price of money includes interest rates and exchange rates, you can begin to appreciate the importance of the subject to you and your work.

Unfortunately, many people try to study economics by using their memories rather than trying to understand the general principles. Understanding how prices are determined and what affects them is far more important than memorizing formulae. There is a similar need to understand, rather than memorize, the general principles of law and accountancy.

Technology

Technology is increasingly important for banks, which now have major communications networks for their computers. In the 19th century, communications technology meant the railway and the telegram. Then came the telephone, typewriter, adding machine, accounting machine, computer, photocopier, cash dispenser and facsimile (fax) machine. Home and office banking are two developments that are likely to become more widespread in the next few years. Virtual banking, whereby all the facilities of a branch are available from home computers, is a virtual certainty this century! Without first-class technology, a bank, no matter whether it is retail or wholesale, cannot hope to compete to keep and enlarge its share of the market – or even enter the market.

Marketing

The last word of the last paragraph was 'market', a place where buying and selling occurs. Marketing is a term used to describe the effort which businesses put into designing and selling goods and services which: (a) customers need, and (b) can be sold at a price which gives reasonable profit to the seller.

Marketing is not 'selling'. Anybody can sell something at a loss; hardly anybody can sell an item that a customer does not want. It takes hard work to devise something which can be sold, at a profit, so that the customer, or customers, come back for more.

Adapting

To enjoy life and to succeed, a person must be adaptable and be able to change. This does not mean being weak and agreeing to everything but being able to realize that we cannot expect things to stay the same for ever. For instance, the business we join in 2002 will change dramatically before we are 40, ie before 2026, and again before we retire in, say, 2044 – assuming that we stay with the same employer!

Not only must we adapt to change but so must banks, if they are not to become financial dinosaurs on the way to extinction. Change may come from law – new Acts of Parliament and court judgments; from politics and economics – the European Union and the single market; or from technology – electronic accountancy and funds transmission.

Changes in communication

To give an example, the current law on cheques is based largely on an Act of 1882, when cheques were transported by steam train and the telegram was the fastest means of communicating. Today, cheques go by road if at all, and e-mail is the 'state of the art' in communication. The cheque is now becoming less popular for drawing cash from bank accounts as more people use cash dispensers each year, while direct debits are increasingly used to make payments.

Changes in the law

Changes in the law can affect banking and other financial services in several ways:

- Decisions of the courts, in both the UK and the European Union.

- Acts of Parliament and European Union legislation.

Changes in money

To give another example, many of us used phonecards, which are a way of paying in advance for our telephone calls from public phone boxes. In Japan, phonecards are so popular that they are given as presents and the telephone company has received so much money in advance payment of phone calls that the government looks upon it as a sort of bank. The next step is to extend the use of these cards to, say, buying newspapers and bus and train tickets. At present, an exhausted phonecard is thrown away, but you do not have to be a day-dreamer to realize that a re-usable plastic card could be the money of the 21st century.

Trials have been made of a new form of cash – 'electronic purses' or 'electronic wallets' – which are much like plastic cards with built-in memories but which can be 'topped up' with money balances from special telephones (at home) or from special cash dispensers (in the street or banks). One of these trials – of a card called Mondex – was held at Swindon while, in the area around Leeds, trials were made of a rival card called Visacash. These cards are intended to be used for quite small purchases, such as bus fares or car parking or buying newspapers, but the necessary equipment will have to be installed to read the cards and to deduct the price being charged from the outstanding balance in the card's memory.

Changes in banking

The pace of change in banking has begun to accelerate since about 1960 when changes in information technology began to initiate what some commentators have called the Information Revolution. During the preceding Industrial Revolution (about 1760 to about 1960), the banking system in England and Wales became very centralized with the evolution of the big five clearing banks and the spread of the 'banking habit' to most sections of the population rather than being restricted to the wealthy few. This process took almost two centuries, concluding with the merger in 1968 of two of the big five to form Nat West, so that there were only four major retail banks.

Today, the position of the big four is being eroded as the information revolution enables new competitors to enter the retail banking market. New entrants do not have to purchase or construct expensive buildings for use as branches in which to house their clerks and cashiers. The employees are located in enormous data processing centres – often on a trading estate where land and rents are cheap. Moreover, not all new entrants offer all the services sold by the big four. Current accounts are often not available from the new competitors. Customers contact the new entrants not by physically visiting the offices but by phone, e-mail or post. Customers are now able to do business by using the Internet – the Internet is no longer mainly a source of information about the ranges of products available.

Marks & Spencer were the first new competitor, but they offered only PEPs, pensions and their credit card (confusingly called a charge card and which is reserved for use at their stores!).

After M&S had 'tested the water', the first wave of new competitors were the building societies, beginning in July 1989 when the Abbey National Building Society became a bank with its shares quoted on the London Stock Exchange. Its name is Abbey National plc. (Plc stands for public limited company, as you will see in Chapter 8). Other building societies have moved in the same direction, either by being taken over by a bank or merging and then becoming a bank.

The second wave were the supermarkets, often in tandem with a retail bank – Sainsbury's (Bank of Scotland), Tesco (Nat West and then Royal Bank of Scotland), Safeway (Abbey National), Asda (LloydsTSB) and Morrisons (HSBC). Asda and Morrisons are pursuing a policy of allowing their partner banks to open branches in some of their stores. The other three larger supermarkets are running telephone banking operations, with savings accounts as their core products as well as credit cards and/or mortgages.

Next were some life assurance companies – Scottish Widows, Legal & General and Standard Life – selling telephone savings accounts and sometimes mortgages. One of the latest new entrants is Egg, partly owned by Prudential Banking plc, a member of the insurance group. It is a part-telephone, part-postal bank, with paying-in and ATM facilities at branches of the HSBC Bank.

To some extent, this entry of life assurance companies into banking was a mirror image of the earlier entry of retail banks and building societies into selling insurance policies, particularly those needed by personal customers – life, house, car and travel insurance. However, banks tended to avoid marine and aviation insurance, just as insurance companies' banks have avoided – so far – competing for business accounts. Following this wider product range for both banks and insurance companies, the term 'financial services' came into common use.

Finally, a number of American banks have reinvigorated the market for credit cards, sometimes offering low 'teaser' rates of interest for up to six months to entice cardholders to transfer their debit balances from their existing banks. The entry of these banks has given a new lease of life to credit cards which seemed to have become what is called a 'mature' market in the early 1990s.

Another possible change will come from Economic and Monetary Union (EMU) which, after being implemented fully in early 2002, will create a single currency for eleven of the members of the European Union.

The Business of Banking

This is the title of this book, which introduces the reader to some of the rules, procedures and problems faced in day-to-day banking. These relate mainly to retail banking, because that is where most bank employees work and where most people have their bank accounts. Banking may be unique in that it is so intimately involved with money, but it is not unique in the fact that it faces competition in selling its services – or products as they are often known – to customers. It is just like any other business because it needs to make profits to survive. For a definition of a bank, readers must wait until the beginning of Chapter 7, however, because it is rather complex.

Summary

We can remember the eight vital features of banking by the acronym:

METAL LAMP

These letters stand for:
Money
Economics
Technology
Accountancy
Lending

Law
Adapting
Marketing
People

- *Money* is the stock-in-trade of banks and if new assets are used as money in the future then the banks must be involved.

- *Economics* shows how interest rates, exchange rates and other prices and policies are determined.

- *Technology* determines the practicalities of day-to-day operations.

- *Accountancy* is used in controlling the banks' business and in assessing requests to borrow large sums of money.

- *Lending* is a very profitable and a very risky activity of banks.

- *Law* governs the relations between banks, their customers, their employees and their shareholders (owners).

- *Adapting* is necessary for survival.

- *Marketing* is necessary if what banks sell is both popular with the customers and profitable for the banks.

- *People* are always important.

Further Reading – Chapter 1

Anderton B (Ed), (1995) *Current Issues in Financial Services,* Chapters 1, 5 and 9. Macmillan. ISBN 0 333 56799 4.

Heffernan SA, (1996), *Modern Banking in Theory and Practice,* Wiley. ISBN 0 471 96209 0.

Croft, Norton, Whyte (1999), *Management in the Financial Services Industry*, Chapters 1, 4 and 9 (the latter is vital for students – who must manage their time). CIB Publishing. ISBN 0 85297 502 3.

2 Money

Objectives

After studying this chapter you should be able to:

☐ Outline the history of money.

☐ Explain the four functions of money.

☐ State the seven characteristics that help it perform these functions.

☐ Define money, liquidity and the various assets that comprise today's money.

☐ Outline the ways in which the UK government measures the stock of money.

A world without money

First, there wouldn't be any pay days! Instead, we would all receive some of what we were producing and then we would try to swap it for what we needed. For instance, if we were bakers, living in the time before money was developed, we would try to exchange our loaves for clothes, drink, fuel and shelter. Let us consider the many problems that we would have:

- To clothe ourselves we would need to find a tailor who actually wanted a loaf or two of bread: technically, this is a double coincidence of wants. Not too difficult, you might say, but nobody would swap a dress or a coat for one or two loaves of bread. How many scores of loaves would you exchange for one dress for an average-sized person?

- We would then need to agree an exchange rate, say 144 loaves to one standard-sized coat. But the tailor could not eat 144 loaves at one go. So we might agree to deliver the loaves over a five-month period – deferring the supply of them.

- Our loaves would soon go stale, so we would have to swap them within 48 hours of the baking. Lucky old tailors or dressmakers – at least they can hang their products in a cupboard for a month or two! They can store their products.

- Our loaves cannot be stored – for freezers haven't been invented – so we have another problem: how can we put things by for old age or for when we are ill and cannot work? The answer must be that we must bake more loaves, swap them for clothes, fuel, etc, and then save these items until we need them.

Probably, we would spend such a long time swapping and storing these commodities that the time remaining for baking – our main occupation – would be much reduced.

Not surprisingly, societies throughout the world developed money. At first, popular commodities such as animals were used to determine the rate of exchange and which goods were swapped. For instance, one sheep might equal five loaves and one standard-sized coat equal 30 sheep. We still swapped the loaves and the coats but in ratios related to their value in sheep.

Later, people began to see an advantage in swapping goods via their sheep price not directly but indirectly, ie into sheep first and then out of sheep into what was really needed. This brought another problem: sheep are difficult to carry – try carrying three or more! Also they do not last forever, although far longer than a loaf; they cannot be divided like a loaf and some are bigger or healthier than others.

So, people changed from using animals as a primitive form of money to using precious metals. The latter could be carried easily, were quickly recognizable and could be divided. Moreover, they lasted much longer than animals. Societies now had reached a form of money which would be an asset used for swapping goods and services and paying debts.

A brief history of money in England and Wales

The earliest forms of money were animals, shells and precious stones and metals. In Tibet they even used 1kg tablets of tea!

In Britain they had begun to use copper and tin coins just before the arrival of the Romans, who brought with them their own coinage, usually silver. When the Romans left, the use of money ceased. Soldiers were paid in grants of land and peasants paid rents in land services.

You may be asking: 'Where do the banks fit in?' A good question, but we must bear in mind that money is far older than modern banking. Primitive banks can be traced to 2000 BC but it was not until the 11th and 12th centuries AD that active banking emerged. In England, banking at that time tended to be in the hands of Jews, who looked after rich people's money and lent it, often to finance crusades.

But finance for a risky project, such as war, carries a high rate of interest and the unpopularity of the high rates charged by the Jews led to their expulsion from England in 1290. They were replaced by Italian immigrant bankers, from Lombardy, who settled in a part of London which still bears their name – Lombard Street.

These bankers later became known as goldsmiths, because they dealt in gold, which first entered the European monetary scene in the 16th century from the Americas. Previously, gold was too rare to circulate as money. These goldsmiths looked after rich people's gold, giving the depositors a receipt.

Eventually, people who had these receipts found it easier to exchange them for goods and services than go back with the receipt to the goldsmith for some money. Thus, the goldsmith's receipts were becoming more like what we know as banknotes. However, the receipt was usually for an awkward amount eg fourteen pounds eleven shillings and nine pence (about £14.59) and was made out to a person, ie the banker promised to pay A. Richman the sum of £14 11s. 9d. on demand. The banknote, however, is made out for a round sum, eg £20, and the banker promises to pay 'the bearer', who is the person bearing or holding the note, rather than A. Richman or some other named person.

Gradually, these early bankers realized that not all their receipts or notes would be presented at any one time, so they began to lend some of their stocks of gold to earn a profit. There were two problems arriving from this development:

- Some of the loans might not be repaid

- What happened if more of the noteholders asked for their money back than the banker had expected?

Matters would be made much worse if news got around – and banking was a local activity – that a trader had been unable to continue his business, leaving unpaid debts with a local banker. That banker's noteholders would rush to get their money back, in case the banker couldn't continue in business. This is known as a 'run on a bank' and causes serious problems for the bank concerned.

The solution is to borrow, if possible, from other bankers or from any organization that is able to act as lender of last resort. Unfortunately, until the 19th century there was no lender of last resort and most local banks would be unwilling to become involved with the 'distressed' bank for fear of being dragged down with it.

During the 19th century, most privately owned banks surrendered their rights to issue notes to the Bank of England, which is a special type of bank known as a central bank. Central banks are often closely linked to the government of the country where they are situated, and may act as this special lender of last resort to the banking system in general and, often secretly, to 'distressed banks'.

In the first half of that century, there was a vigorous public debate over the principles on which England's money supply – then banknotes – should be based. Eventually, it was decided that, with a small exception, the country's bank notes should be backed by holding a stock of gold or silver, to prevent too many notes being issued. Notes could, of course, be exchanged for gold at the bank that issued them.

An important Act of Parliament, called the Bank Charter Act, was passed in 1844. As a result of the Act:

- The Bank of England could issue notes without restriction, provided they were backed by holding gold or silver bullion, with no more than 20% backed by silver. However, strict limits were placed on the total of notes that the bank could issue which were not backed by gold or silver. This is called the fiduciary issue, because it is based on faith rather than bullion and *fides* is the Latin word for faith.

- The fiduciary issue was fixed at £14m, with increases allowed to enable the Bank of England to take over the note issues lost by private banks. The fiduciary issue could increase by two-thirds of the note issue surrendered by the private bank.

- All other banks were prohibited from increasing their note issues.

- Any bank merging with another bank had to surrender its right to issue notes. This process lasted until 1921, when all the private banks had ceased to issue notes.

Thus, bank notes replaced coins as the major part of the nation's money. But, while the Bank of England was gradually dominating the note issue, as the note-issuing banks lost their powers of issue, other great changes were occurring.

First, bank deposits became much more important, being transferred from person to person by means of cheques. The Bankers Clearing House in London began in 1770 to handle these cheques.

Second, the tax on cheques, which had been a percentage of the amount of the cheque – usually 1% – was changed in 1855 to a flat 1d (roughly 0.42p) for each cheque. This made cheques much less expensive. Just over a century later, in the run-up to decimalization, the tax was abolished.

Third, the completion of most of Britain's railways enabled cheques to be sent to London overnight so that transit time was enormously reduced.

Fourth, the Bills of Exchange Act 1882 gave statutory protection to banks handling cheques, provided certain conditions were met.

So, if you're wondering, 'Why didn't banks resist the surrender of their note-issuing powers?' then here is the answer. They did not need to issue notes because their customers could use current accounts and transfer parts of the balance by writing cheques.

The World Wars changed matters dramatically. In 1939, as World War II started, the whole of the Bank of England's note issue became fiduciary, because the Bank's gold was needed to buy weapons from the USA.

In 1949 the fiduciary issue was £1,500m and in 2001 it was £28,000m. In the UK, we now use the American terminology and a term a thousand million a billion, which is often abbreviated to 'bn'. So, the fiduciary issue is £28bn. But bank deposits are many times that amount, and so are building society deposits.

That was the history of money until a few years ago, when plastic entered the scene! Plastic cards are now more popular than cheques for withdrawing cash from bank accounts and are slowly competing with cash and cheques for the purchase of goods and services.

Probably just as important has been the growth of building societies to be so powerful as to compete head-on with the established banks for people's business. This process of interlinking and competition between banks and building societies is likely to continue during this century. By then, the pace of change may have slowed, but the 'plastic' revolution may really be under way, as very sophisticated plastic cards replace much of our coinage, banknotes and cheques. Also, we may have one kind of money for the whole of the European Union.

The functions of money

It's back to theory now, using the problems we met in the first section of this chapter on *A world without money*. Money's task is to solve these problems, which it does in four ways, which are given special titles. Money acts as a medium of exchange, a liquid store of value, a unit of account and a standard of deferred payments. Let us take each function in turn.

A medium of exchange

Instead of swapping goods for goods – a process known as barter – we exchange goods for money and then the money for other goods. Money acts as an intermediary.

Earlier in this chapter, we noticed the problems of finding someone who wants to swap exactly what you have to swap – a problem technically known as the double coincidence of wants. Money overcomes this problem easily.

Without all the exchanges of goods and services made possible by money, we would have to be much more self-sufficient and hence endure a lower standard of living. The division of labour, which you may study next year in economics, is virtually impossible without money.

Money – such as notes and coin and credit balances on current accounts, which act largely as a medium of exchange – is sometimes called narrow money.

A liquid store of value

Do you remember the problem our baker had trying to save loaves for his or her old age? The use of money can largely overcome this problem because money is always worth its face value. For instance, a pound will always buy a pound's worth of goods or services, providing prices do not change too much – and that is very important. Money is a reasonably liquid store of value, by which we mean we can save it and spend it fairly easily, unlike loaves.

We use the word 'liquid' because most bank and building society deposits can be very easily changed into notes and coin: without delay, without any cost and with no loss of capital value or interest forfeited. And that is the definition of liquidity – a characteristic of an asset which is able to be converted into cash quickly at minimum cost and with minimum loss. Try selling a second-hand car and see how much hassle there is with such an illiquid asset! Houses and company stocks and shares can often be good stores of value, for old age or sickness, but they are highly illiquid.

Money such as deposit and savings accounts in banks and building societies, which is used largely as a liquid store of value, used to be called near-money or quasi-money (*quasi* means partly). However, these days when many more balances can be drawn upon demand (or sight as it is called technically), this near money is included with narrow money to form broad money. Another technical term for near money is time deposits because up to 90 days' notice may have to be given to withdraw the credit balance if interest is not to be forfeited. These ideas can be shown diagrammatically (see Fig.1).

Figure 1
The major functions of money

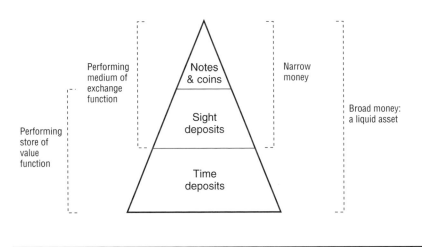

You should ask, 'How can sight deposits perform both major functions?' The answer is that today banks pay interest on more and more of their sight deposits (current accounts in credit) while building societies have always paid interest on all their deposits. Interest is the reward for saving and makes interest-bearing accounts very attractive liquid stores of value.

Using money to save, ie not spending it, enables the country to build hospitals, schools, factories, motorways, railways, bridges and even the Channel Tunnel. These are all items that we do not consume quickly – unlike food and drink – and they should last for years to enable us to enjoy a better standard of living.

A unit of account

Suppose our baker baked cottage loaves, rolls, cakes and sponges. If we asked him: 'How much did you sell last week?' He might reply, '460 cottage loaves, 380 rolls, 470 cakes and 60 sponges'. Or he could have said 'Sales came to £930'.

We use money to add together all sorts of completely different items, for reasons of clarity and brevity, to help us to calculate:

- Total values of all the assorted articles;

- Figures for the profit or loss we have made on the transactions in the past year;

- Budget totals of expenditure beyond which we may not go in the coming year;

- Forecasts of sales/profits which we expect to achieve during the coming year.

In other words, and not surprisingly, we are using money for accounting, management information and targeting – a sort of measuring rod.

A standard of deferred payments

Do you remember our baker, trying to buy a coat and eventually agreeing to supply 144 loaves over a period of five months? In effect, he was using the loaf as a standard of deferring payment for the coat over this period.

We do not do anything like that. We defer payment by offering to pay money, usually over a much longer period than five months. For instance, we might borrow money to buy a house, repaying the original amount borrowed, together with interest, over 25 years. Or we might rent a flat for a period of five or seven years, paying monthly or quarterly rentals in advance. After that, the rent will probably be changed, with a larger amount usually being demanded by the landlord.

Here we are using money for banking and legal purposes, incorporating money values in the contract.

You can remember the functions of money by the word **SUMS**:

Standard of deferred payments
Unit of account
Medium of exchange
Store of value

The last two are the most important.

The characteristics of money

These are sometimes called the qualities of money. They are frequently confused by students with the four functions we have just described. They are the qualities that must be possessed by assets if they are to function efficiently as money. The assets are coins, notes, bank deposits, and building society deposits. We touched on some of the qualities in the first section of this chapter, *A world without money.*

There are seven qualities and it is not easy to remember them all just like that. So, teachers have devised a phrase to help you remember these qualities – SPUD RAD.

Imagine a potato on a radiator- a SPUD on a RAD (!). Each letter stands for a different quality, each ending in the letters *-ity*.

Stability of value and scarc*ity*
Portabil*ity*
Uniform*ity*
Divisibil*ity*
Recognizabil*ity*
Acceptabil*ity*
Durabil*ity*

Stability and Scarcity

Stability of value is very important. The value of money is what it will exchange for (buy, in other words) and if it buys less goods and services tomorrow than it does today then it is not performing its four functions very well.

In the next chapter, you will study the problems resulting from inflation – a rise in the general level of prices – and the causes of it. If money halves in value each month then it is pretty useless for saving, for incorporating in contracts, or to do bookkeeping. The only thing to do with it is to spend it immediately.

Stability of value is associated with scarcity. If we use gold as money and new goldfields are discovered, then the amount of money, ie gold, increases and so do prices. If we print more banknotes, then prices will rise. If we allow banks to acquire more deposits – more about this later – then prices will rise. If we use chickens as money and there is a plague which kills them, we have a shortage of money and prices fall. So, we do not want too rapid a rise or fall but some stability in prices and values.

Portability

Remember when we discussed trying to carry three sheep? Does your purse or pocket bulge with £1 and 50p coins? Ever been abroad and seen the larger notes they sometimes use in other countries or had a fistful of Italian notes?

You must be able to move money around easily. Literally that means carrying it but it also means transferring it by cheque, telex/telephone or plastic card.

Here we must point out that a cheque is not money. A cheque merely transfers a bank balance from person to person, unless it is dishonoured by the bank and returned marked 'Refer to Drawer'. That does not happen with banknotes and coins!

Uniformity

Each unit of money must be identical with every other in size, appearance and weight. Banknotes are uniform, except some are cleaner than others. Each bank deposit is uniform because we trust the bank that holds the deposit.

But this uniformity has not always existed. In Tudor times, there were rogues who literally 'clipped' small particles of metal from coins, melting down the particles when sufficient had been collected. This clipping meant that many coins contained slightly less precious metal than he or she should have done and people were reluctant accept such coins. Once somebody received such a clipped or debased coin, they spent it as rapidly as possible. This tendency for 'bad' money to be spent more rapidly than 'good' money is known as Gresham's law, after Sir Thomas Gresham, the Elizabethan financier. Only by ensuring that all the units of money are identical and of the same value can a government avoid Gresham's law.

Another name for uniformity, used in some textbooks, is homogeneity.

Divisibility

Our live sheep could not be cut into portions and still be alive. Money is not affected by this problem because we have a system of change, with notes and coins of differing amounts – notes of £50, £20, £10, £5, coins £2, £1, 50p, 20p, 10p, 5p, 2p and 1p. Using these we can make up different amounts of money.

With bank and building society deposits we can pay in any amount of money, subject to any minimum deposit requirements. We can withdraw any amount up to the balance of the account, subject to any restrictions as to minimum period of notice of withdrawal and minimum amount. With a cheque book we can transfer part of our deposit to a third party; we do not have to use whole pounds when we write a cheque because this can include pence too. Thus we can write a cheque for £999.99, if required, and are not restricted to a choice of £990 or £1,000.

Recognizability

We must be able to recognize money instantly as being money and not confuse it with, say, tokens or luncheon vouchers. Not only that, we must be able to distinguish a 5p coin from a 20p and a £10 note from a £50 note. In the UK, this is achieved by size, shape and design of coins and notes. This is not so in the USA, where all banknotes are the same size and colour.

Acceptability

This quality is very important. Today, £50 notes are still not completely acceptable for fear of forgeries and a number of petrol stations have notices stating they will not be accepted. Again, builders who often pay cash for their supplies from builders merchants prefer to be paid in £20 notes rather than £50 notes.

Acceptability is even more important for bank and building society deposits and any assets such as an electronic wallet which may become money in the future. In the 19th century, few people had bank accounts, so that payment by cheque was used only by the wealthy. Today, the majority of people have bank accounts and even more have building society accounts, so they are prepared to accept cheques, provided they are sure that the cheques will not be returned unpaid.

In 2002, when euro notes and coins began to circulate on the Continent, the acceptability of this new money was very important in ensuring the smooth changeover.

Durability

Money must last. Coins must not become too worn and notes must not become tattered. Notes, however, have a short life. The Bank of England has to replace all our £5 notes about once every twelve months. This makes printing all these notes very costly.

Bank deposits are very 'long-lived' because a credit balance with a bank does not have to be repaid until the customer requests it, as we shall see in Chapter 7. If the customer forgets about the balance on the account, the bank does not. After a period of say four or five years of not hearing from a customer and having letters from branches returned marked 'gone away', such 'dormant balances' are transferred to head office, with full details of the balance, customer's name and last known address. Building societies have different procedures because, technically, each customer is a member of the society and bound by its rules.

Money, liquidity and assets used as money

Money is an asset

Money can be defined as any asset generally accepted in payment of debts.

Asset is a word which is much wider than commodity, including not only the animals, beads and metals used centuries ago but also coins, notes and bank and building society deposits. In accountancy, an asset is defined as the property or possession of the owner. Animals and commodities are real assets, because you can see them and touch them. Bank and building society deposits cannot be felt and can be seen only as entries in a ledger, statements or on a screen. Such assets are called intangible.

Another aspect of bank and building society deposits is that, while they are assets in the accounts of the customers, they are liabilities in the accounts of the banks and building societies themselves. This 'double role' arises from the basic principle of double-entry bookkeeping.

Acceptability is very important. In the UK we are, at present, happy to accept notes, coins, bank and building society deposits expressed in sterling. But, if prices doubled overnight, we might prefer to accept chocolates or the money of a foreign country, such as US dollars or Swiss francs.

Liquidity

Liquidity is that quality possessed by an asset which enables it to be converted into money without:

- Delay
- Cost
- Loss of value or interest

We can change our bank deposits into cash today but it may take six months to sell our house. If we have a 90-day notice bank account, then we either wait 90 days or lose 90 days' interest.

In these days of free banking, it does not cost us anything to withdraw money from our bank, apart from time, shoe leather, petrol, parking fees or bus fares. Selling a house could cost us over £200 in solicitor's fees and far more in commission to the estate agent who sells it for us.

With banks and building societies we know that we will always get back the face value of the account if we withdraw the balance in it. However, with houses, stocks and shares and many other assets you may get less or more than you hoped you would get.

Some National Savings products are liquid, but others are not, because encashment requires either considerable notice or the loss of interest. One such illiquid product is National Savings Certificates, which must be held for a complete period of three months, after the first year, to receive any increase in capital value.

Money today

Today, money comprises:

- Coin

- Banknotes

- Bank deposits

- Building society deposits

Some of these assets are legal tender – by law we must accept them if they are tendered (offered) in payment of a debt. This law is imposed by the Coinage Act 1970, which states that the following coins and notes are legal tender for the stated amounts:

Bronze coins	1p, 2p	for amounts up to 20p
Cupro-nickel coins	5p, 10p, 20p,	for amounts up to £5
50p coins	50p	for amounts up to £10
Pound coins	£1, £2	for any amount
Bank of England notes	£5, £10, £20, £50	for any amount

Notice that Scottish and Northern Irish banknotes are not legal tender and neither are bank deposits and building society deposits.

Legal tender is a form of money which we must accept by law if it is tendered or offered to us in payment for something. Money is an asset which is generally – not legally – acceptable when offered in payment for something.

Measuring the stock or supply of money

The definitions are decided by the Treasury and the Bank of England – known as 'the authorities' – and the statistics are published monthly by the Bank of England. They bear numbers, rather like motorways, and also have colloquial names. They exclude money (notes, coins, deposits) held by

- the government,

- banks and building societies,

- overseas residents.

The important measures are M0 and M4. Every so often, changes are made with some measures being altered, others abolished and sometimes one or two are renumbered. Major changes took place in 1987, after the Building Societies Act 1986, and again in 1989 after the Abbey National became a bank. The latter change caused the disappearance of the M1, M3 and M3c measures, which may feature in books written before 1989.

M0

M0 is also called the wide monetary base, comprising notes and coins held by the public – 'you, me, ICI and BP'.

This money is in our pockets and in the tills of shops, and in the safes and cash boxes of offices throughout the country. It includes:

- Notes and coins with the general public.

- Notes and coins in the tills and cash dispensers of the banks and building societies.

- The operational balances of banks at the Bank of England (At present, not all building societies maintain such accounts at the Bank of England).

M0 is often regarded as the major measure of narrow money (see above).

M4

M4 is the major measure in the UK of broad money, which we defined above. It comprises:

- Notes and coin with the general public (the first part of M0).

- All deposits in sterling from UK residents with banks and building societies.

So, when we pay our taxes to the government by deduction from our salary or by cheque, the money supply falls (by definition). When the government pays the wages of civil servants, the money supply rises. When sterling is used to pay foreigners for the goods we import from them, the money supply also falls.

These are just some of the topics you will touch upon in economics.

Summary

- Without money we would have the problems arising from barter – the need for a double coincidence-incidence of wants, change, agreement on value and the need to exchange goods within a short period of time. Money solves all these problems.

- Originally animals and commodities, money has comprised coins, notes, bank deposits and now building society deposits. Soon plastic and electronic money will become important.

- Money has four functions: a standard of deferred payments; a unit of account; and the two major ones which are a medium of exchange and a liquid store of value. SUMS is a memory aid.

- Assets used as money must have seven qualities if they are to function efficiently as money: stability, portability, uniformity, divisibility, recognizability, acceptability and durability (SPUD RAD should help you to remember them).

- Money can be defined as any asset generally acceptable in settlement of debts.

- The speed with which other assets can be converted into money depends upon their liquidity. Only certain forms of money are acceptable as legal tender.

- When the assets used as money fulfil the functions of money effectively, the country can enjoy the extra output this makes possible by investing in roads, hospitals, etc, and is able to improve profit planning and budgeting and credit.

- Money is measured by the government, which publishes several measures of the stock of money, according to how liquid, or easily convertible into note and coins, each asset is. The important ones are M0 and M4.

Further Reading – Chapter 2

Molyneux, P, (1993) *Banking: An Introductory Text*. MacMillan. ISBN 0333541197.

3 More about money

Objective

After studying this chapter you should be able to:

- [ ] Explain how money is created.

- [ ] Demonstrate how 'every bank loan creates a deposit'.

- [ ] Identify the roles of banks, the government and people overseas in creating money.

- [ ] Define the value of money.

- [ ] Calculate changes in its value.

- [ ] Explain why inflation is regarded as so harmful by the government.

- [ ] Show how interest rates and exchange rates are the price of money.

- [ ] Identify the main goal of the government's monetary policy.

- [ ] Show why people save and how people use money and other assets to save.

How money is created

The country's stock of money comprises largely notes and coin and bank and building society deposits, as we saw in the previous chapter. We also noted that, by definition, those M numbers which measure the quantity of money exclude money held by banks, building societies, the government and overseas residents.

So, we have a clue as to the source of more money – banks, building societies, the government and overseas residents. Let us take each in turn.

Banks

At the beginning of the previous chapter, we saw that the early bankers began to lend the gold that they had received from their customers, because not all their notes would be presented at one time. A summary of a banker's accounts might be along these lines:

	£		£
banknotes issued in return for gold deposited	1,000	Gold in vaults	300
		Loans to customers	700
	£1,000		£1,000

The borrowing customers would have taken much of the £1,000 of gold originally deposited.

But there are further stages in this process because the borrowed gold would mostly come back to the banker – particularly if he were the only one in town – when the borrowers spent their gold in the local shops. The shopkeepers would then pay it into their bank – his bank. Then his accounts might be:

	£		£
banknotes issued in return for gold deposited	1,500	Gold in vaults	800
		Loans to customers	700
	£1,500		£1,500

Every loan creates a deposit

Of the £700 lent, £500 has been re-deposited at the bank, so that the banker has now issued £500 of new notes. As part of the double-entry bookkeeping, the 'contra' item is the £500 increase in the gold in the vaults. This brings the total of the banker's gold to £800. None of this is earning any interest to pay his expenses, so he will consider increasing his loans, which earn interest, and running down his gold stock.

The next stage is this extra lending, with loans rising by £500 to £1,200 and gold holdings falling to £300. His account would then be:

	£		£
banknotes issued in return for gold deposited	1,500	Gold in vaults	300
		Loans to customers	1,200
	£1,500		£1,500

The following stage is when much of that borrowed gold returns, so that the accounts read:

	£		£
banknotes issued in return for gold deposited	1,900	Gold in vaults	700
		Loans to customers	1,200
	£1,900		£1,900

As you can imagine, the process can be repeated many times, with the increase in banknotes gradually getting smaller because not all the money lent returns to the bank.

Spreading the risks

In practice, our banker will also be concerned that he possesses only gold and loans and so he will soon be considering possessing other items, such as securities issued by the government. These will still yield interest and have the advantage that the risk of the government not repaying the capital sum is far less than that of a borrower not repaying his or her loan.

The accounts will then look like this:

	£		£
banknotes issued in return for gold deposited	1,900	Gold in vaults	500
		Loans to customers	1,200
		Government securities	200
	£1,900		£1,900

Hopefully, the £500 of gold in the vaults will satisfy the customers who are exchanging their banknotes for cash, while the £200 of securities can be sold if the gold holdings fall significantly.

The banking system

You may be thinking 'What happens if there are three or four banks in the town? Not all the gold withdrawn by borrowers will return to our banker – perhaps only a fifth.' Well, you are right, because if one bank 'goes it alone' and lends, its loans will end up as deposits with rival banks.

However, if the examples were to refer to a banking system, ie all the banks in a country, in which all the banks expand their lending at roughly the same rate, then the same thing might still happen.

Most of the lending will return to the banks, with only a fraction being held elsewhere in cash – perhaps in people's mattresses! – or being paid to the government, eg in tax or to people overseas. Do not forget that money held by the government, and by banks and foreigners, is not included in the M measures of the quantity of money.

So, the banking system is a sort of 'closed circuit' with entry only from banks, the government and from overseas. Which brings us to the role of the government.

The government

'Of course the government creates money. It, or strictly the Bank of England, issues our notes, and the Royal Mint issues our coins.' If you have said this, then you are correct but there is more in this than just issuing notes and coins.

Taxation and spending

Whenever we pay our taxes, such as VAT on goods we buy, the money leaves our wallets, purses or bank accounts and eventually reaches the bank accounts of the government at the Bank of England. These taxes, when received by the government, are excluded from the money supply. So, when people pay taxes, the money supply falls.

But the government does not sit on this money paid in taxes – it spends it. When pensioners, teachers, soldiers, students, etc receive this money, their cash or bank deposits rise, and those of the government fall. It is the reverse of tax collecting, so the money supply rises.

Now comes a big 'if'. If the amount raised in taxation and the amount spent by the government are exactly equal, then the combined effect of taxation and spending is nil, because the increase in one cancels out the increase in the other. Money supply is unchanged.

If you say, 'Nonsense, they are never equal, because the government is always spending more than it raises in taxes', then, surprisingly, you are only half right. Let us see.

Government borrowing and debt repayment

When the government spends more than it raises in taxation, it has to find the money from somewhere. It borrows it, from those people who buy National Savings Certificates or Premium Bonds or put money in the National Savings Bank, and also from pension funds and life assurance companies that buy government securities – called 'gilts' – on the Stock Exchange. 'Gilts' is short for 'gilt-edged', meaning they are of the highest quality, with no risk of interest not being paid or of default on repayment of the original loan. Let us see what happens when somebody buys £100 of Premium Bonds, or a pension fund buys £10m of gilt-edged securities from the Government.

The purchaser of the Premium Bonds pays £100 in cash or by cheque over the counter of a post office. His or her bank deposits fall by £100 – as does the money supply – and the government's holdings of money (which are excluded from the money supply) rise by £100. So, money supply has fallen.

It is much the same with a pension fund, only the amounts involved are far larger. The pension fund buys the gilts from the Government with a £10m cheque drawn on its bank account; its credit balance falls, as does the money supply. The government's balance at the Bank of England rises by £10m, but the money supply does not increase, because of the definition stated above.

Therefore, we can say that if the government borrows money from the general public, businesses and financial institutions, this has a contractionary effect on the money supply, in the same way as when taxes are collected.

Overseas residents

Again, relying on the government's definition, if bank deposits flow into the UK from overseas holders, then the money supply rises. For instance, if UK exporters are very successful in their sales, more pounds will be sent to them by their foreign purchasers. When the exporters' bank deposits rise, so does the UK's money supply.

With imports, the opposite occurs, because UK importers sell pounds to buy currency to pay the foreign exporters. If the pounds are then bought by foreigners or UK banks, then the UK money supply falls.

In the 16th century, the Tudors suffered inflation which was partly caused by silver and gold being shipped to England from South America. The money supply rose as these metals were minted into coins, and it rose faster than England's production of goods and services.

Another aspect of overseas transactions is 'suitcase' money, literally carried in suitcases on airlines from country to country.

The value of money

We all know the value of items such as a car or a stereo system – it is the money which we paid for it or which we hope to get if we sell it. The values of goods are expressed in money.

What about the value of money? Is the value of a £20 note represented by another £20 note or four £5 notes? Of course not. If we think for a bit, we can see that the value of money is the goods and services we can exchange for it. Another phrase for this value of money is the purchasing power of money.

Inflation and deflation

As we suggested in the previous chapter in the section on stability of value, money is a measuring rod of value for goods and services which can change, sometimes quite rapidly. In June 1989, prices were rising at 8.3% a year, so that they would double every eight or nine years. But in Argentina, prices were doubling every month, with disastrous results. By October 2001 UK prices were rising at only 1.6% a year, so that they would double only every 21 years. And in Argentina, prices were *falling* at about one per cent a year.

Inflation in a country causes people to move away from that country's money, wherever possible, and into assets such as houses, gold, stocks and shares and foreign currency. Inflation benefits borrowers, because they pay back their loans with money which buys a great deal less (is worth a lot less) than the money they borrowed. Inflation hurts lenders, who receive less in purchasing power than they lent to the borrowers and hurts all who have their income or their capital (savings) fixed in terms of money, which buys less each month.

However, money does not always fall in value, because prices do not always rise. Sometimes, deflation occurs as prices fall and the purchasing power of money (its value) rises. The last time this happened in the UK was between 1920 and 1935, when prices fell and miners, civil servants, the police and the armed forces had to accept cuts in pay. The 1926 General Strike was in support of a miners' strike against wage cuts. Even bank clerks had their annual salary rise cut from £15 pa to £10 pa!

If you say, 'That was a long time ago' then you are right but you must remember that prices can and do fall as well as rise. After 1989, the prices of most houses fell substantially and only later started rising again.

Paintings and other works of art can fall in value as well as rise, and here fashion and demand can affect prices substantially.

Causes of inflation

Inflation has many causes and economists often disagree as to which are the more important at any one time in a particular country. However, three main causes can be outlined:

1. Demand-pull inflation, where buyers bid up the prices of goods and services.

2. Cost-push inflation, where sellers have to increase prices because their costs – wages, raw materials and fuel (especially oil) – have risen.

3. Structural inflation, where a country's wage bargaining and price determination are so organized that an easy solution to problems is to raise prices.

Measuring inflation

Inflation can be measured by measuring the changes in the prices of goods and services. The trouble is that there are thousands of shops and millions of transactions each week. We cannot record each one centrally! So, the government organizes certain samples in order to publish a range of statistics called index numbers, in which the prices of (say) food and housing are more important than the prices of clothing and perfume. There are several indices:

1. General Index of Retail Prices (known as the headline RPI), which uses January 1987 as its base or starting point. It is calculated once a month and published on a Tuesday in the middle of the following month.

2. Underlying inflation (called RPIX), which is headline RPI excluding interest paid on mortgages. This is the measure which is targeted by the Government to be 2.5% pa in about two years' time.

3. Tax and price index, also monthly, which seeks to take into consideration the changes in take-home pay caused by income tax and national insurance contributions. It tries to measure the purchasing power not of money but of take-home pay.

4. Index numbers of producer prices: (a) materials and fuel purchased, (b) output. These indices seek to measure changes in prices of items long before they reach the shops or are exported.

5. Average earnings index, which is usually published about three or four days before the RPI. Our earnings are important for two reasons – we spend them and so influence prices; our employers pay them and so will try to raise prices in order to recoup their extra costs when earnings rise.

If the RPI rises by 10% in a twelve-month period, then the value of money falls by almost the same amount – an eleventh or 9.1%. The arithmetic is:

$$\frac{100 \times 100}{110} = 90.9$$

$$100 - 90.9 = 9.1$$

If prices double then the value of money is halved:

$$\frac{100 \times 100}{200} = 50$$

Index-linking

To help those people affected most when prices rise substantially, the governments of some countries have introduced what is called index-linking. This phrase means changing the monetary value of assets and incomes by the same extent as the rise in one of the indices we have just mentioned. The most important example in the UK has been the annual increase in the state retirement pension (the old age pension) and many other social security benefits, which occurs every April. Until recently, these were increased in line with the annual increase in the RPI to the preceding September.

The other examples of index-linking are too numerous to mention, but they include TV licences and some National Savings Certificates. Even the interest-free student loans have their principal amounts index-linked to the RPI.

Index-linking, however, does not eliminate the causes of inflation. It merely lessens its effects on people.

Exchange rates and interest rates

As we saw when we discussed the functions of money, there are other things we can do with it apart from spending it in the UK. For instance, we can exchange it for the money of other countries, using a price called the rate of exchange. The rate of exchange of £1 in early January 2001 for European currency was about €1.62 – this is another way of saying that the cost or price of £1 bought by a holder of European currency was €1.62.

Money's second great activity, apart from being spent, is being saved or, to use the words of the previous chapter, as a liquid store of value. We can save money by simply storing it in a cash box under the bed, but if we deposit our cash in a bank or building society we can earn interest on it.

This rate of interest is the price or cost of money to the borrower, whether he or she is in the UK or overseas. However, if the borrower is resident overseas, he or she has another way of acquiring pounds – buying them in exchange for another currency on the foreign exchange market. This possibility of choosing between borrowing pounds on the money markets or buying them means that interest rates and exchange rates are closely linked, as traders switch from currency to currency and market to market to seek the most attractive returns on their funds. Usually an increase in interest rates in a country leads to a rise in the exchange rate of its currency, as more people buy it, unless the foreign exchange markets lose confidence in that currency.

Links with inflation

These can be complex. When prices in the country rise, the government may seek to raise interest rates to restrain people from spending. This rise in interest rates will cause foreigners, attracted by the higher yield on their funds, to buy that currency and so raise its exchange rate.

Also, savers will require higher interest rates as some compensation for the loss of purchasing power of their savings.

Unfortunately – just like the boy who cried 'wolf' so many times that nobody bothered when the wolf really came – increasing interest rates too many times may have the opposite effect. If inflation is surging ahead, then foreign investors may take fright and sell that currency, even though interest rates have been raised.

A country with a high rate of inflation can usually sell its exports if it makes them cheaper, by lowering the exchange rate (the price) of its currency to compensate for the high cost of its exports. For instance, if the price of a £10 toy made in the UK rises to £12 then, at €1.62 to £1, its cost in European currency rises from €16.2 to €19.44. This increase may cause European buyers to buy from a cheaper foreign or European competitor.

To get the toy's price back to €16.2 needs either cheaper methods of production in the UK, which may be impossible, or a change in the exchange rate to €1.35. Such a sudden drop may cause foreigners to sell pounds, irrespective of the level of UK interest rates, but there is no doubt of its other effect – European goods priced at €1.62 will no longer sell at £1 in the UK but at £1.20, thus raising prices again (unless the sellers reduce their profit margins).

Investors may, therefore, view higher interest rates and high inflation as signs that a fall in the exchange rate of that currency against other currencies is likely to occur. This means that the purchasing power of their funds invested in that currency is likely to fall, so they sell before it does. But their sales will probably result in the currency's exchange rate falling – so they bring about the events from which they seek to escape!

Interest rates, exchange rates and inflation are extremely complicated and difficult – disputes over what the UK government should do about them caused Mr. Lawson to resign as Chancellor of the Exchequer in October 1989. And, before 1997, the Chancellor of the Exchequer and the Bank of England sometimes disagreed about whether or not to change interest rates. If they cannot get it right, then banking students should not despair if they find it difficult. But you won't be asked such complex questions in most examinations!

Monetary policy

Monetary policy is how the government tries to improve the country's economy by using banks and money, acting on the level of deposits and loans, and on interest rates and exchange rates.

As well as keeping inflation low, a government will seek to keep unemployment low and output rising. However, it cannot do all three things at the same time. For instance, if it is very successful in lowering unemployment, the shortages of workers may cause wages to rise, as employers bid for more employees. The workers will spend their increased wages in the shops and this may cause prices to rise – thereby causing inflation to rise.

A government may have to choose therefore between these aims or goals. Recent governments chose the reduction of inflation as the goal that should be given the utmost priority. Unemployment, economic growth and the enormous gap between exports and imports were not considered so important.

Forms of monetary policy

There are many different ways of carrying out monetary policy.

Controlling the banks' assets

During the period 1940 to 1980, the commercial banks often had tight controls placed on their assets – on what they did with their deposits. For instance, from time to time 'ceilings' were placed on the amount of loans that any bank could make.

Another form of control was to require all banks to place a 'special deposit' at the Bank of England, which could not be included as a liquid asset (forcing them to 'save' this money).

Yet another version of control was to have an overall ratio of liquid assets to deposits – sometimes up to 28%, and then, in the 1970s and using different definitions, down to 12.5%.

Money supply targets (later monitoring ranges)

The use of targets declined during the 1980s, so that by early 1990 the only measure of money targeted was M0, which was supposed to grow at a rate between 1% and 5% in the twelve months from March 1990 to March 1991.

The government later had monitoring ranges for M0 (0% – 4% pa) and M4 (3% – 9% pa), which were to continue beyond 1997. However, these monitoring ranges are now no longer used in the UK, although the Germans still preferred to have money supply targets until the European Central Bank became responsible for monetary policy in 1999.

Fixed exchange rates

From October 1990 to September 1992, the government fixed the exchange rate of sterling at DM2.95, while the UK was in the EU's Exchange Rate Mechanism. The aim was to reduce inflation, but speculators forced the UK out of the ERM in a spectacular crisis.

Interest rates

By the end of the 1980s, the government's sole weapon of monetary policy was the general level of interest rates charged by banks and building societies. The Bank of England, acting under powers given to it in May 1997, can change banks' base rates by changing the rate of interest at which it lends as lender of last resort. This is said to be a 'signal' to all banks to change their most important rate of interest – their base rate, which is used to calculate the interest charged on many of their loans. Their other loan rates, and the rates given on deposits, will follow – in the same direction but not all simultaneously. Eventually, the new interest rates affect all lending and borrowing except existing transactions at fixed rates of interest.

After the UK left the ERM in 1992, attention had focused on the monthly meetings between the Governor and the Chancellor – at which the Chancellor decided whether or not base rate should be changed. These meetings ceased in 1997, following the general election and the new Chancellor's decision to give operational responsibility for changing short-term interest rates to a new Monetary Policy Committee at the Bank of England. This Committee meets monthly and the minutes of the meetings are published on the Internet and in hard copy a fortnight later. The Bank now publishes a quarterly Inflation Report.

Inflation target

This became the UK's current form of monetary policy in 1992 and has been redefined several times since then. The target today is decided by the Chancellor of the Exchequer (as monetary policy targets always have been) and is to achieve an inflation rate of 2.5% per annum in about two years' time, using short-term interest rates as the main instrument to reach this goal. The decisions as to what level of short-term interest rates is necessary to achieve this target are taken each month by the Monetary Policy Committee of the Bank of England, and not by the Chancellor of the Exchequer. If the target is not reached by a margin of plus or minus 1 per cent (ie, inflation is under 1.5% pa or over 3.5% pa) then the Governor must submit a report to the Chancellor.

European Union monetary policy

Operational decisions are taken by the European Central Bank, using a three-pronged approach:

1. an inflation target of 2% or less;

2. a monetary reference range, a measure of broad money;

3. a mix of other economic indicators.

It, too, changes short-term interest rates.

Fiscal policy

As we saw earlier, the difference between a government's expenditure and tax revenues will affect the money supply, so this aspect of government activity is very important to banks and to the money markets.

However, a government can influence an economy more directly by, say, constructing new motorways or giving teachers or nurses a substantial pay rise. These activities – spending, taxing and borrowing new debt or repaying old debt – make up a government's fiscal policy.

Saving

In short, saving can be defined as 'not spending all our income on goods and services'. If we all did this, there might be problems but we can be sure that there are also people who are doing the opposite – spending more than their income. Hopefully, the under-spenders should equal the over-spenders, but they rarely do!

Reasons why people save

Young people are not known for being great savers but examiners are always older than their candidates and older people often save more. So, in an exam about financial services, you might well have a question on the reasons for saving. These are as follows:

Future expenditure
There is often a very important reason to save for: a holiday, a deposit on a car or a house, a wedding, etc. The feature of this type of saving is that expenditure can be predicted. Some parents take

out life assurance policies shortly after their children are born for a private education or an eventual wedding.

For emergencies
These are the events whose dates or even occurrence cannot be predicted. Sickness or a car breakdown cannot be forecast and can be quite unexpected. Some money put by for this 'rainy day' will be very useful, and a target of three times monthly gross income is often recommended for this purpose.

For the family
As parents get older, or become grandparents, they begin to think of providing for the younger family members to give them 'a start in life'. This motive could be important, for instance if house prices continue to rise rapidly, placing homes beyond the finances of young borrowers.

Tradition
Some people are traditionally thrifty. They may continue to save even when inflation is much higher than the interest rate they receive from their savings.

For an increase in wealth
Less spending today should mean more wealth and more income in the future. This motive is a deliberate decision by the saver to try to become richer.

To establish a track record
If people can show that they can save a reasonable sum each month, then lenders will be more disposed to grant credit to them.

For old age
With people living longer and retiring earlier, more of us will need to be saving harder (during a shorter working life) for a longer old age. Moreover, the Government is concerned about the cost of state provision for older people, so that we cannot rely on our retirement pensions as our parents may have done. Personal pensions (including stakeholder pensions', ISAs and rental income from

property) are three possible means of achieving a reasonable future income.

To fulfil a contract

If you have a life assurance policy or a personal pension, then you have a legal obligation to put the premium or the contribution aside and to pay it to the insurance company or pension fund. These contractual savings can be very important because they are not dependent on the whim of the saver.

How people save

At first, people's holdings of money will rise when they save: they will have extra money in their purses or wallets, and larger balances at their banks and building societies. Banks and building societies will compete fiercely with each other for people's savings but they will also compete with unit trusts, life assurance companies and pension funds. If customers are paying 5% of their salary to their employer's pension fund then they may have less need for other forms of saving.

We can group the various forms of saving into four:

1. Balances at banks and building societies, and also more cash at home.

2. Financial assets, eg stocks and shares; unit trusts.

3. Financial contracts, eg life assurance policies, pensions and regular savings schemes with unit trusts. Banks and building societies no longer draw much attention to their own regular savings schemes.

4. Real assets – things that are your property and which you can touch, such as 'bricks and mortar'. These include a bigger home or a second home in the country for weekends and/or holidays, as well as jewellery and antiques.

Summary

- Money, in the form of bank deposits, is created when:

  a) Banks make more loans to domestic borrowers

  b) The government spends more than it raises in taxation

  c) Money flows in from overseas.

- The value of money is what each pound will buy in goods and services. This is also called the purchasing power of money.

- Price changes are measured by a price index. As the index rises, so the purchasing power of money falls.

- Inflation is a period of steadily rising prices and has several drawbacks: it is harmful to savers, people on fixed or slowly-rising incomes and exporters. The latter will compete with goods from countries with much lower inflation rates.

- Inflation can be caused by excess demand (demand-pull); rising costs (cost-push); or by traditional ways of fixing prices and wages.

- Prices and wages can be increased in line with inflation by linking them to a price index – usually retail (shop) prices.

- This index-linking softens the effects of inflation but does little to remove the causes, and inflation can become traditional for a country.

- Exchange rates are the price of buying (and selling) our currency, expressed in foreign currencies.

- Interest rates are the prices of borrowing (and lending) our currency, and are charged to both UK and overseas borrowers.

- Exchange rates and interest rates are closely linked: usually a rise in a country's interest rate causes its exchange rate to rise.

- An exception to this is if inflation is so high that overseas investors lose faith, and sell the currency, thus forcing down its exchange rate.

- Monetary policy is one way in which the government seeks to contain inflation and unemployment. Fiscal policy is another.

- Today, UK monetary policy relies increasingly on interest rates, ignoring more direct controls once used on banks and their lending.

- Saving is: not spending all your income on goods and services. The unspent money can be placed in banks or building societies, or used to buy stocks and shares, life policies, pensions.

- People save for many reasons: future spending, emergencies, for the family, for future wealth, for their old age, to get a credit rating or to fulfil a contract.

Further Reading – Chapter 3

Lipsey RG and Chrystal KA, (1995), *An Introduction to Positive Economics*, Oxford University Press. ISBN 0198774249, 8th ed, Chapters 35, 36 and 38.
    Bank of England Inflation Report, ISSN 1353 6737.
    The Report's Overview is available on:
    www.bankofengland.co.uk/inflationreport/ infrep.htm
    The entire Report is on:
    www.bankofcngland.co.uk/inflationreport/index.htm

4 The recent history of banking and finance

Objectives

After studying this chapter you should be able to:

- [ ] Outline banking history up to 1951.
- [ ] Display more detailed knowledge of events since then.
- [ ] Explain how the Bank of England has developed.
- [ ] Discuss the importance of building societies.
- [ ] Describe markets for banking products.
- [ ] Outline the background to the great changes of the last 15 years.
- [ ] Examine the rationale for the Banking Acts of 1979 and 1987.

1694-1950

In 1694, the Bank of England was founded for a special purpose – to lend money to the King for a war against France. In return for this risky loan, the Bank had the right of being the only joint-stock company (ie owned by shareholders like companies today) allowed to be a bank and issue notes. All other banks had to be partnerships or sole traders. The monopoly of the Bank of England was reinforced by an Act of Parliament in 1709 which restricted the members of a banking partnership to only six.

So, in the 18th century, banknotes were issued by a large number of small banks and by the Bank of England. Gradually, cheques were introduced and in 1770 the Bankers Clearing House was founded. At about the same time, the Industrial Revolution, which started in the Midlands and North of England, caused the growth of a large number of small banks.

Towards the end of the Napoleonic Wars in 1815 a great debate began on the structure of England's money supply – notes and coins in those days – and on the structure of the banking system. In 1816 the UK went onto the Gold Standard, whereby all banknotes were exchangeable into gold. This meant keeping enough gold in the Bank of England vaults to repay the notes which it had issued. The UK remained on the gold standard for almost a century until the outbreak of World War I in 1914.

By 1844, most major cities were linked to London by railway, enabling the national cheque clearing system to develop. The use of cheques was encouraged by the flat rate stamp duty (tax) of one old penny per cheque after 1855. Before then, the duty was based on a percentage of the amount of each cheque. By 1866 there were 154 joint-stock banks, but the merger process grew, so that by 1900 there were 77 and by 1914 only 16. In comparison, in 1900 there were more than 2,000 building societies.

During the 19th century, the discount market developed into something approaching its 20th century role, ie as a cushion between the Bank of England and the rest of the banking system. Also, many of the leading merchant banks became established in their traditional role of financing international trade. Both depended on bills of exchange, used to finance domestic and international trade (these will be discussed in later chapters), but the joint-stock banks depended increasingly on cheques and bank deposits. The discount houses and the merchant banks were closely controlled by the Bank of England.

At the end of World War I in 1918, the government appointed the

Colwyn Committee to report on bank mergers. Its report, recommending no more major bank mergers, governed the authorities' attitude to bank mergers until the end of the 1960s.

By the end of 1918 there were 11 clearing banks, compared with 17 in 1917 and this total remained 11 until 1968.

The 1920s were a decade of expansion, with the 'Big Five' – Barclays, Lloyds, Midland, National Provincial and Westminster – all seeking new business, mainly opening branches in towns where they were at that time unrepresented. The Midland was then the largest – in fact the largest bank in the world.

The 1930s, however, were a period of contraction as the century's worst economic recession occurred. Bank profits fell, recruitment was cut back and some branches were closed.

The 1940s were a decade of war and rationing, with 'exchange control', which had been introduced in 1939, very important. Exchange control is a method of rationing a country's reserves of gold and foreign money (eg the amount you can take abroad) and is still used by many countries today. However, the UK abolished it in 1979.

In 1946, the Bank of England was nationalized.

1951-1970

In the autumn of 1951 a Conservative government was returned to power and gradually dismantled the apparatus of controls created during the war. Interest rates, which had remained low since 1931, partly to contain unemployment and then to provide cheap finance for the war effort, were raised in order to prevent inflation from rising.

The banks began to compete with each other again and local authorities were freed from borrowing solely from the central government. This allowed a new financial market to develop – the local authority market where the authorities borrowed from banks and wealthy companies and people. German, Japanese and Italian banks began to return to the City of London. The Bank of England regulated the eleven clearing banks mainly by a liquidity ratio of 30% which was lowered to 28% in 1963, but this constraint did not apply to the many other banks in the UK, nearly all in London. This freedom to keep a lower liquidity ratio gave these other banks a competitive advantage over the clearing banks.

You will recall the definition of liquidity from Chapter 2. In the early 1950s, the clearing banks' liquid assets were mainly notes and coins, balances at the Bank of England, and assets traded on the discount market. However, at the end of the 1960s, banks regarded their loans to the new money markets as liquid assets.

In about 1958, the Bank of England indicated that it would allow banks, but not the clearing banks, to accept deposits in foreign currencies as well as sterling. At first, these deposits were in US dollars, but other foreign currencies soon featured, as what became called the Euro-currency market developed. A Euro-currency has little to do with the European Union but is a currency deposited and lent outside its country of origin.

Some five years later (about 1963) a further new market began – in deposits and advances in sterling in London, between banks themselves rather than between banks and their customers. This is the inter-bank market.

The attraction of operating in these two markets caused a large number of foreign banks to open branches in London, in addition to those banks which had been present since the previous century.

In 1966, a new instrument, or document, was introduced. This was the certificate of deposit (CD) which acknowledges the deposit of money for a fixed period of between three months and five years. If the holders want their money back before then, they sell it in a secondary market. At first, CDs were only for US dollar deposits in London but sterling CDs were first issued in 1968. Clearing banks could not issue them until 1971.

The clearing banks, although shackled by their 28% liquidity ratio, were active. In 1965 they began issuing cheque cards, with a £30 limit, and in 1966 Barclays launched Barclaycard. However, the banks' interest rates were uniform, in spite of the very attractive interest rates paid by building societies which were becoming very popular with the general public as a 'store of value'.

In 1962 the National Provincial Bank had bought the District Bank, but allowed it to trade independently. In 1968 the merger of National Provincial with Westminster was announced, changing the relative positions of the Big Five. National Provincial and

Westminster were the fourth and fifth largest but the new National Westminster was about equal to Barclays, which in 1955 had overtaken Midland to become the largest UK bank.

Barclays and Lloyds had, separately, each been seeking to buy Martins, a smaller clearing bank with its head office in Liverpool, and their reaction to the Nat West merger was to propose a three-way merger. The government was concerned, referring the bid to the Monopolies Commission which, in the summer of 1968, recommended that Martins merge with one but not both of the bidders (thus preventing a three-way merger). Barclays then took Martins and, therefore, the Colwyn report became out of date.

On the operations side, computers came into general use just before the currency was decimalized in 1971. Also, improvements were made to the clearing of credits (not cheques) in response to the creation of a new bank in 1968 - the National Giro. Later, this became known as the National Girobank and, later still, Girobank plc.

1971-1985

In 1970 a Conservative government had been elected and set about a policy of change. In 1971, the Bank of England published a document called *Competition and Credit Control* which included uniform rules for all banks, thereby enabling clearing banks and all other banks to compete under the same rules, or what was once termed 'a level playing field'. The liquidity ratio was dropped and a new reserve asset ratio of 12.5% was created while each bank chose its own structure of interest rates, based upon its base rate.

The problem was that the rules had to fulfil two distinct functions:

(a) to control banks and prevent them acting recklessly, and

(b) to implement the government's economic policy of keeping inflation and unemployment at low levels. Eventually, in 1980, the Bank of England introduced two distinct sets of rules, one for each purpose.

With their new freedom to compete, the clearing banks and others lent heavily, especially to commercial property borrowers, in what was then the greatest post-war boom for most of the world. When the OPEC (Organization of Petroleum Exporting Countries) raised oil prices in 1973-4 the boom burst and interest rates soared. Some newer banks, which were not supervised by the Bank of England, had lent a great deal of money to failing property companies and began to lose their deposits in the inter-bank market. The Bank of England organized a rescue operation by the clearing banks, known as the Lifeboat. All these 'fringe' banks have been either wound up or rescued from the Lifeboat, which no longer exists.

This secondary banking crisis was one reason why Parliament passed the Banking Act 1979, giving the Bank of England legal powers rather than persuasive powers to prevent banks from acting imprudently. Another reason was that in 1973 the UK had joined the European Economic Community, which required a comprehensive statute regulating banks. The Act divided the banking community into full-blown banks and licensed deposit-takers. Unfortunately, one of the full-blown banks (Johnson Matthey Bankers) collapsed in 1984, and the 1979 Act had to be replaced by another.

In 1980 the rules of Competition and Credit Control were withdrawn. Since then the Bank of England has deliberately avoided using ratios to implement the government's economic and monetary policy, working instead via the day-to-day interest rates in the money markets.

1980 also saw some, and later all, of the clearing banks move into lending for home loans as a frontal assault on the building societies' core product – mortgages for owner-occupiers. At about this time, the various local and regional trustee savings banks were being grouped into four national TSBs, before being floated as a public limited company in 1986 and known as TSB Bank plc.

1986 to date

This is the period when the rate of change began to accelerate. Moreover, some of the changes in the first part of the period were reversed in more recent years.

The economic background was one of swings in interest rates and asset prices (shares, bonds and houses) but, towards the end of the century, inflation was contained and interest rates then fell to lows not seen since the 1960s. House prices, which fell in the early 1990s, causing 'negative equity' (owing more on the mortgage than the house was worth), were rising steadily as the fourth edition of this book went to press. Share prices, however, were lower at the start of the new century than they had been in the late 1990s.

The political background was one of growing concern for personal saving, witnessed by the number of Acts of Parliament mentioned in this section and by the development of tax-efficient savings products. There were a number of problems – misselling of personal pensions in the late 1980s, the failure of many endowment policies to grow sufficiently to repay the mortgages of the homeowners who had taken out these policies, and the difficulties of the oldest life assurance company – Equitable Life – caused by lower interest rates and its failure to maintain adequate reserves (so as to have generous bonuses for its policyholders).

The social background was one of an increasingly elderly population, so that provision for old age is becoming very important. A side-effect is that older people are slower to change to newer forms of 'product delivery' such as the Internet, preferring to use bank branches and sub-branches. Banks tended to close branches and new branches were very rare. Staff recruitment dried up and 'downsizing' was the norm as costs were pared to increase profits.

In 1986, the Financial Services Act was passed, establishing a group of Self Regulatory Organizations for the participants in the financial services market to regulate themselves. These five SROs then became three, whose regulatory role was taken over by the Financial Services Authority on 1 December 2001, when the Financial Services and Markets Act 2000 came into operation. Ten years ago, the letters FSA stood for Financial Services Act, whereas they now stand for Financial Services Authority. Self-regulation is now far less important than it was ten or fifteen years ago.

Also in 1986, the London Stock Exchange was reorganized ('Big Bang' it was termed), with the ending of the distinction between jobbers (traders) and brokers (buying and selling agents for shareholders) along with the end of the prohibition of banks owning jobbers and brokers. The aim was to enable London to compete with the exchanges in New York and Tokyo. Many but not all banks bought member firms of the stock exchange, while others contented themselves with providing share-dealing services for their customers.

Another important Act in 1986 was the Building Societies Act, which has led to a number of the largest societies becoming public liability companies, often with their shares traded on the London Stock Exchange where they now tend to be called 'savings and mortgage banks' or just 'mortgage banks'. The first to become a PLC was the Abbey National in 1989, but in 1996 and 1997 there was a veritable stampede of societies becoming PLCs – some, such as the Bristol & West (bought by the Bank of Ireland) and Birmingham Midshires (bought by Halifax in 1999) did not issue shares to their investing and borrowing members, who got a cash payment instead. The Halifax itself had taken over and absorbed the Leeds Permanent Building Society in 1997, and in 2001 it merged with the Bank of Scotland to form HBOS plc. However, both the Halifax and the Bank of Scotland continue to do business under their old names. The Woolwich, which had four years of independence as a PLC, was taken over by Barclays at the end of 2000, although its brand name has been retained. Another society that has disappeared from the high streets is National & Provincial, which was absorbed by the Abbey National in 1997.

In 1987, the Government introduced the first of a series of tax-efficient investments – Personal Equity Plans (PEPs). In 1991 came Tax Exempt Special Savings Accounts (TESSAs). In 1997, the Labour Government announced changes to the regime of tax-efficient investments. These changes were implemented in 1999, when new PEPs and TESSAs could no longer be opened. Instead, there were Individual Savings Accounts (ISAs) – which come in one or more of three types – along with TOISAs (Tessa Only ISAs for re-investing the capital portions of TESSAs maturing after their five-year lives). PEPs continue, although new ones cannot be opened.

1987 was an important year for a number of reasons – two of which caused problems to the banks affected. The first problem was the debt rescheduling by a number of developing countries, particularly in Latin America. Many banks had lent substantial amounts to such countries in the late 1970s and early 1980s and writing-off these loans caused heavy losses to these banks. Another problem was a short but sharp fall in share prices in the autumn of 1987 – Black Monday, it was called. The fall resulted in losses in their stock exchange business and many banks withdrew from such transactions.

By the end of the 1980s, banks were heavily involved in stock exchange business and mortgage lending – two new areas. As we have seen, some banks have withdrawn from trading on the stock exchange but mortgage lending is still very important. However, one development in the late 1980s did not last for more than about eight or ten years – purchasing chains of estate agents so as to sell banking products such as insurance (now very important), loans and budget accounts along with mortgages. The falls in house prices in the early 1990s meant that the volume of house sales achieved by estate agents fell substantially and most banks sold their loss-making estate agents. Lloyds Bank sold Black Horse Agencies to Bradford & Bingley, making it and the Halifax the only banks to own estate agents' chains.

Until the middle of the 1990s, most banking and building society mergers resulted in the disappearance of one or both of the brands involved. Thus, NatWest Bank (later to be just NatWest) had been formed from District, National Provincial and Westminster and, of course, it is more than a generation (30 years) since Martins Bank traded as such. However, the practice at present seems to be to try to preserve brand loyalties – hence we have Bristol & West, Lloyds TSB (a twin brand formed from both these banks which merged most of their operations in the late 1990s), Woolwich (now owned by Barclays Bank) and Birmingham Midshires (although a number of branches have been closed after the takeover by Halifax), not forgetting Cheltenham & Gloucester (bought by Lloyds Bank in 1994). One proposed merger that was not approved by the Government was in 2001, when Abbey National and Lloyds TSB wanted to combine. This was rejected because it would have diminished competition.

The 1990s also saw a number of new entrants to the banking and financial services markets – from insurance companies such as Scottish Widows (later to be taken over but not absorbed by Lloyds TSB), Standard Life, supermarkets (often linked with existing banks

– Sainsbury's {Bank of Scotland}, Tesco {Royal Bank of Scotland}) –
and outsiders such as Virgin. Such new entrants were not burdened
by the high costs of a large branch network, often operating from
'call centres' on industrial estates. They provide telephone banking
rather than counter service and in some cases have Internet
facilities.

Banks have not been slow in providing Internet facilities for
their customers but there have been technical problems in some
cases and there is a tendency to have separate brand names for their
Internet banking services. Thus, Abbey National has Cahoot, the Co-
operative Bank Smile, Halifax Intelligent Finance and the
Prudential still has a majority shareholding in Egg (whose shares are
quoted on the London Stock Exchange).

Of all the years examined in this section, 1997 was the one with
the most changes. Not only did many building societies become
mortgage banks, but the Bank of England was given 'operational
independence' (freedom to change interest rates to achieve the
Government's monetary policy) and the creation of the Financial
Services Authority was announced. However, the legislation was
very complicated and it was not until 2000 that the Financial
Services and Markets Bill became an Act of Parliament. The Act
came into operation on 1 December 2001.

During the 1990s, a number of 'codes of practice' came into
effect. The first (in 1991) was the Code of Banking Practice, then
called 'Good Banking', and the other which most concerns readers
is the Mortgage Code. They still operate, in spite of the overall
supervision by the FSA.

A development that has received little publicity or comment is
the demise of the discount market. All the discount houses have
now ceased business and the Bank of England deals directly with
the banks in implementing its interest rate policy and in its role as
lender of last resort. The market ceased to function in the mid-
1990s. Instead of discounting bills of exchange, banks undertake
sales and repurchases of balances (repos, as they are called).

On the 'plastic money' scene, Lloyds, Midland and NatWest had
launched Access in 1972, to compete with Barclaycard. The Royal
Bank of Scotland and Bank of Ireland soon joined Access but many
smaller banks and, later, building societies joined the Visa network,

to which Barclaycard had become linked. Access, in the meantime, had joined the other international credit card network – Mastercard – under which it now trades. The name 'Access' is now history and the Joint Credit Card Company, whose brand it was, has been wound up.

At the start of the 1990s, many observers thought that the market for credit cards in the UK was saturated, but they were proved wrong when a number of aggressive American banks entered. Also, General Motors launched the GM card, British Gas launched Goldfish, while other new entrants were Sainsbury and Tesco.

The Banking Act 1987 had changed the controls imposed by the 1979 Banking Act, but this did not prevent two further serious crises:

- In 1991, a complex foreign bank known as BCCI (Bank of Credit and Commerce International) had to be closed by the Bank of England as a result of serious fraud. As a result, many large depositors lost much of their money, staff lost their jobs and borrowers had to be sued for the return of their loans.

- In February 1995, Barings collapsed. It was a leading merchant bank, founded in 1762, but one of its employees had engaged in speculative deals in options (technically called derivatives) in Singapore and Japan, incurring heavy losses as a result. The bank was bought by ING Bank, based in the Netherlands. Although the Bank of England had rescued Barings in 1890, it could do little to help in 1995.

Building societies

These date originally from the 18th century, when groups of people set up mutual societies to build themselves houses. When the first house was built, they drew lots to see which member would have it, repeating the process until all the members had a house. The society was then wound up. Gradually, the societies changed in character, admitting investing members whose role was to lend money rather than help build the houses.

As we saw earlier, there were over 2,000 societies in 1900, but by the beginning of 1988 there were 138 and the number may soon fall below 75. The societies merged, just like the banks, into national organizations whose names are very well known, eg the Halifax and the Woolwich – both names revealing local origins.

Societies have, until recently, been 'two-product organizations' – a savings account and a mortgage. They grew larger by paying competitive rates of interest on their accounts throughout the 1960s and 1970s. In 1980, the banks moved into mortgage lending and the societies responded by offering current accounts. But to do this effectively, the societies needed legislation – the Building Societies Act 1986. The Act gave societies additional powers in five major areas:

- Money transmission – current accounts and thus possible membership of the clearings.

- Lending – personal loans and overdrafts of up to £10,000, but only for societies with assets over £100m; other loans must be secured by charges on land.

- Other financial products – purchase of life assurance companies, starting stockbroking subsidiaries and unit trusts, PEPs, and buying up to 15% of general insurance companies.

- Non-financial products – large societies can develop and manage land; move into estate agencies and conveyancing; undertake HP, executor and trust work, share registration, tax and financial planning and advice.

- Wholesale funding – with an overall limit of 40% (now 50%) on the proportion of a society's deposits taken from the wholesale money markets.

As a result, Nationwide Anglia and the Abbey National both launched interest-bearing current accounts, in 1987 and 1988 respectively. Within six months, the Big Four clearing banks had all devised interest-bearing current accounts to avoid losing too many customers to the building societies.

Finally, the 1986 Act laid down a procedure for societies to lose their mutual status, become public companies and thus become banks.

The reasons for a building society becoming a bank may be summarized:

- Access to greater amount of capital, via shareholders and the Stock Exchange and to newer money markets.

- More flexible control from the Bank of England, instead of regulation by the Building Societies Commission under the 1986 Act. Extra powers for societies could need new legislation and this could take up to five years, which was too long in a fast-moving market. However, both banks and building societies now have the same regulator.

- Better remuneration packages for staff. These can now include share options.

- By the mid-1990s, with stagnant house prices and few new mortgages (compared to the heady 1980s), it became apparent that a building society could not grow organically – it had to merge with another society or a bank.

The great disadvantage is the possibility of a take-over, either by a UK or foreign bank. To counter this, the 1986 Act prevents shareholders in a newly converted society from owning more than 15% of the shares until five years after becoming a Plc. The 1997 Building Societies Act stipulates that a converted society, if it takes over another bank or society, loses its immunity from take-over.

Foreign banks

There are now about 550 foreign banks in London, largely to deal in the new money markets which have developed since 1955. At one time, the American banks were very powerful but, in terms of size of deposits and lending, the Japanese banks have overtaken them.

The Bank of England

During the 19th century this had changed from being the country's major private bank to being the country's central bank, with responsibility for:

- Avoiding major crises.

- Lending to the discount houses as lender of last resort.

- The country's note issue.

- Supervising the discount houses and accepting houses.

- Managing the government's day-to-day finances and borrowing (but not directly involved in taxation).

First, the Bank had to have some freedom in the rate of interest that it could charge. This was provided in 1833 when the usury laws were repealed. These prohibited excessive rates of interest by fixing a maximum. Incidentally, it was only relatively recently that such laws were repealed in the Channel Islands and the Isle of Man, permitting them to become international banking centres.

From time to time, there were crises as a bank or banks got into difficulties and the Bank's reaction was to raise its Bank Rate, at which it would lend to the discount houses. The saying was: 'A 7% bank rate would bring money in from the moon!'.

In 1877, the Treasury bill was created. Usually it takes the form of 91-day promissory notes issued by the government, which the Bank of England sells every Friday and which, from time to time, have formed the major asset of the discount market. In the past ten years, the Bank of England has issued new types of Treasury bill, including some for 182 days (six months).

During the interwar period, the Bank of England became increasingly responsible for implementing the government's monetary policy, especially the exchange rate of sterling and the level of interest rates.

In 1939, exchange control was introduced requiring the Bank to authorize all payments overseas, both in sterling and foreign currency, and for all receipts of foreign currency to be sold to it. Much of this work was passed to the banks but exchange control did not disappear until 1979. In 1987, the Exchange Control Act was repealed.

After the end of World War II, the incoming Labour government decided to nationalize the Bank of England as soon as possible. This was achieved by the Bank of England Act 1946, which with the Act of 1998 is the 'constitution' of the Bank today: the Governor and Deputy Governor are appointed by the Prime Minister, each for five years. The other directors are appointed for four years: there are four executive directors, who are very senior officials of the Bank, and ten non-executive directors.

To ensure that the Bank was obedient, the Treasury was empowered to issue directives to the Bank. So far, this power has never been used. In addition, the Bank of England can also issue directives to other banks, subject to the approval of the Treasury. This is a cumbersome procedure and it, too, has never been used.

Until the Banking Act 1979, the Bank did not have any legal powers which it could use on its own. It preferred to use moral suasion, in particular the 'Governor's eyebrows' which if raised (in a manner of speaking) would indicate disapproval. Most banks would immediately cease the activity of which the Bank disapproved.

In 1997, two major changes were announced concerning the role of the Bank of England. Individual banks are now regulated by the Financial Services Authority, as from 1 June 1998, but the other change was implemented within days of its announcement. This was the transfer of decisions on changes in interest rates from the Chancellor of the Exchequer to a new Monetary Policy Committee at the Bank of England, which is now on a statutory basis, under the Bank of England Act 1998.

The growth of the parallel money markets, wholesale banking and the inter-linking of banks and stock exchange firms all caused a great expansion in the Bank of England's functions of prudential regulation of the banking system, overseeing the various new wholesale money markets – where money is lent – and also the foreign exchange market, where money is bought and sold. Today, the Bank of England works very closely with the central banks of the other Western industrialized countries to ensure that all prudential controls are approximately uniform in what is now one world financial market. In other words, the central banks seek to provide that 'level playing field'. However, the Bank of England no longer regulates individual banks, which are overseen by the Financial Services Authority. Nevertheless, the Bank is responsible for the stability of the financial system.

Summary

- In the 18th century banknotes were the greater part of the money supply, being issued by private banks.

- In the 19th century, the note issue was taken over by the Bank of England, but bank deposits became the greater part of the money supply. Joint-stock banks became overwhelmingly important and private banks declined.

- Last century saw the number of banks fall to a low point, but then an influx of foreign banks swelled the numbers operating in the new wholesale markets after about 1958. However, in the retail market, competition came largely from building societies and other new (British) entrants.

- In the late 1980s, two retail banks were floated on the Stock Exchange – TSB and the Abbey National.

- Building societies have grown in importance but fallen in numbers this century. Today, most are minor banks, although they often do not seek business accounts.

- The Bank of England was nationalized in 1946 but this hardly changed its manner of operating, although the Banking Acts of 1979 and 1987 gave it more detailed statutory powers, most of which have passed to the Financial Services Authority.

- Plastic money began with cheque cards in 1965, followed by Barclaycard in 1966 and Access in 1972.

- Self-regulation has been replaced by control by the FSA.

Further Reading – Chapter 4

Piesse J, Peasnell K and Ward C, (1995) *British Financial Markets and Institutions: An International Perspective*, Chapters 13-20. Prentice-Hall.

Moss MS and Russell, I, (1994), *An Invaluable Treasure: A History of the TSB,* Chapters 7-10. Weidenfeld and Nicolson. ISBN 0297 811185.

Ackrill M and Hannah L, (1999) *Barclays The Business of Banking*, Cambridge, 1690-1996. ISBN 0521 790352.

Bank of England, *Practical Issues Arising from the Euro*, Half yearly. London. ISSN 1467 14920.

5 Banks, building societies and insurance companies

Objectives

After studying this chapter you should be able to:

☐ Describe the major importance of major commercial banks as revealed in their balance sheets.

☐ Explain the importance of the inter-bank market for banks' day-to-day operations.

☐ Give the names of the other sterling money markets.

☐ Explain the importance of the foreign exchange markets.

☐ Explain the difference between retail and wholesale banking.

☐ Identify the various classes of wholesale banks.

☐ State the differences between Girobank Plc and the National Savings Bank.

☐ State the essential nature of a building society.

☐ Outline the various types of insurance companies.

☐ Describe the major retail markets where banks, building societies and insurance companies compete.

Introduction

Most textbooks on banking begin with the Bank of England because it is very important, acting as a central bank. However, the Bank's functions now involve so many other financial markets that we are going to study those markets first. We will note in this chapter how the Bank of England is involved and then, at the end of the next chapter, conclude by outlining the functions of the Bank of England to show how it features in nearly all the nation's monetary and financial activities.

In this chapter we examine banks, building societies and insurance companies, most of whose operations take place not in the City but in their branches and telephone call centres all over the country.

Commercial banks

These exist to make profit for their shareholders and now are nearly all public limited companies. They take deposits, in many cases from other banks or from overseas, and lend the money, again in many cases to other banks and overseas.

They have been regulated by the Bank of England, which publishes regular statistics of the balance-sheet totals of all of them. A balance sheet is, in effect, a snapshot of an organization's assets and liabilities – what it possesses and what it owes, respectively – on a particular day.

Because banks do a lot of lending, many of the assets they possess are loans in one form or another and, because they take a lot of deposits, they also owe a lot to their customers. On 31 October 2001 the most important assets of all the banks were as shown in Figure 2.

For a number of reasons, most of which are mentioned later in this chapter, the Bank of England has changed the statistics for banks. However, another very important reason is the creation of the single currency (the euro) and a single monetary policy for the countries using the euro. The UK, although not in the first wave of countries joining the single currency, has adopted the concept of 'monetary financial institutions' (MFIs), which are basically banks and building societies. Accordingly, all the latest data are for these MFIs, either for banks and building societies separately or on a consolidated basis whereby the assets and liabilities are netted out when banks and societies are dealing with each other rather than with the rest of the economy.

MFIs have been defined by the European Monetary Institute (the forerunner of the European Central Bank) as:

> *credit institutions as defined in Community Law, and all other resident financial institutions whose business is to receive deposits and/or close substitutes for deposits from entities other than MFIs, and, for their own account (at least in economic terms), to grant credits and/or make investments in securities.*

The figures for the UK, although lacking in much detail, are very large, with totals of assets (which equal the total liabilities by the rules of bookkeeping and which are known as 'footings') of £3,044,899m.

Figure 2
Assets of MFIs as at 31 October 2001

	Sterling £m	Foreign Currency £m
Loans	1,246,292	1,243,069
Securities (other than futures/ options etc)	117,185	360,158
Other assets	49,910	28,286
Total	1,413,387	1,631,513

Source: Financial Statistics, 2001

These assets – or possessions – are financed almost entirely by bank deposits of one kind or another. Only about 8% come from capital, the money which a bank or company owes to its shareholders and which is repayable only if the bank or company goes into liquidation – 'goes bust', as it is colloquially put.

For the MFIs' liabilities, (see Figure 3) the Bank of England reports the following figures as at 31 October 2001:

Figure 3
MFIs Liabilities as at 31 October 2001

	Sterling £m	Foreign Currency £m
Deposits etc	1,213,565	1,499,564
Other liabilities	200,035	131,787
Total	1,413,600	1,631,331

Source: Financial Statistics, 2001

Deposits

Deposits are the money which has been lodged with the bank and the depositors of a bank are its major creditors to whom it owes money. As we shall see in Chapter 7, there is a special legal relationship between banker and customer when the customer is the creditor.

Because most of our transactions with banks are in sterling, that is where we shall focus our attentions. Let us look at each item in turn:

Sight deposits

These used to be known as current accounts but they comprise all the money deposited with banks which is repayable on demand or at sight. Thus, they include all the instant savings and high-interest cheque accounts which are now so popular. They also include all the deposits taken on the inter-bank market repayable on demand.

Time deposits

These are all those deposits which need notice to be given to the bank before the customers can have their money back. They include the once popular 7-day branch deposits and the now popular 90-day notice investment accounts.

Certificates of deposits (CDs)

These are documents issued by banks and, since 1983, by building societies, acknowledging that a large sum of money has been deposited – £50,000 is the minimum – for a period of between seven days and five years. During this period, the bank which issued the CD is under no obligation to repay it. Thus, the holder cannot present it for repayment but may sell it in a secondary market, in which the nine discount houses (discussed in the next chapter) play a minor role.

Capital

Capital is the money which the shareholders or owners of the bank or business have to put into it and which the business is liable to repay to them should it cease operations, and then only after all the bank's or business's other debts have been paid in full. It also comprises past profits or surpluses (eg, from property revaluations) which belong to the shareholders.

Assets

Assets are possessions – what the bank owns or what it can claim from other people, firms or other banks. Some assets are instantly usable or liquid while others may prove to be worthless. We shall look at the most important types of assets in the order of their liquidity. Liquid assets are marked '(L)'.

Notes and coins (L)

These are held in the cash dispensers, tills, vaults and cash centres of the banks – mainly the retail banks. When the banks want more notes and coin, they ask their bank – the Bank of England – for these! Their accounts at the Bank fall and their holdings of notes and coin rise.

Balances at the Bank of England (partly L)

At £2bn, these are much smaller than holdings of notes and coin but, in spite of their relatively small size, they are extremely important. They are of two types: operational (L) and compulsory cash ratio deposits.

The importance of operational deposits arises not only from their ability to be 'cashed' for notes and coin but because they are used to pay taxes and money borrowed by the government. Also, when the government pays civil servants' salaries etc, these balances rise momentarily. Like notes and coin, these balances yield no interest or income for the banks that own them. These operational deposits, which are maintained by retail banks at the Bank of England, are also used to settle outstanding amounts each day between the banks at the various clearings, described in Chapter 10.

They are separate from the cash ratio deposits, which all UK banks and building societies with over £400m of deposits must lodge at the Bank of England, according to a formula of 0.15% of their sterling deposits from domestic customers, excluding inter-bank deposits. Cash ratio deposits, although they comprise about 80% of the banks' balances at the Bank of England, are not liquid assets. However, operational deposits are liquid assets.

Market loans (L)

These are very important because they act as a 'top-up' to replenish the banks' balances at the Bank of England. Interest is earned on them.

They comprise largely unsecured market loans, mainly in the inter-bank market. Included here are each bank's holdings of certificates of deposits (CDs) issued by other banks and building societies. The major interest rate in the sterling inter-bank market is LIBOR (London Inter Bank Offer Rate) which is used to calculate interest rates on loans to large company (corporate) borrowers and as a measure of the cost of funds raised in the inter-bank market.

As well as the inter-bank market there are other wholesale money markets: CDs, local authority, finance house, commercial paper (CP) and inter-company. As you might expect from its name, the inter-company market does not involve banks directly, because all the parties are companies, put in touch with each other by brokers. The companies use their banks only to process their cheques and not to provide the finance.

Commercial paper is much like a CD, except that it is usually issued by a company whose shares are quoted on the stock exchange and with a paid up share capital of at least £25m. Banks, building societies and local authorities can also issue CP.

Bills (L)

These are mainly commercial bills, eligible (that is, approved) for discount at the Bank of England. A bill is bought and sold at a discount below its face value until the day it matures, when its face value – say, £100,000 – is paid to the last purchaser. His or her profit arises from the fact that he paid less than £100,000 for it. You may ask 'How much less?' The answer depends on the rate of interest because the holder could have invested the money and obtained the market rate of interest on it instead of buying the bill.

Let us take an example, with interest rates at 6%. If a bank buys (or discounts to use the technical term) a £10,000 bill which has three months to maturity, then the bank will pay about £9,852 for it. After three months, it will receive £10,000 which is about 1.50% more than the £9,852 invested. When 1.50% is multiplied by 4 to make three months into one year, the annual rate of interest is about 6%.

Treasury bills, issued by the government, are also important. There are also very small numbers of local authority bills. These bills can be discounted quite quickly but there is one disadvantage – their value will fall if interest rates rise. Try the calculation for yourself: how much would you pay for a three-month £10,000 bill if interest rates were 4%? (The answer is at the end of the chapter).

Advances

An advance is another term for lending, which can be by overdraft or loan. These advances are the largest asset of the banks, the most profitable and the most risky. Hence, banks try to achieve as wide a spread of borrowers as possible between personal, company and overseas customers.

The assets we have examined in this section are listed in decreasing order of liquidity and increasing order of profitability. Cash, for instance, actually costs money to hold, move and insure, but a retail bank cannot operate without it. On the other hand, the riskier an advance, or the more troublesome it is, the higher the rate of interest which is charged.

Investments

Traditionally, banks hold part of their assets in British government marketable securities – gilts as they are known. Such holdings provide a virtually guaranteed source of income and, if held to maturity, the repayment of the nominal value of the security. For instance, a bank might pay £1m for a 10% stock priced at 95 (ie £95) and maturing, ie due to be repaid, in 2006.

The £1m buys £1m x 100/95 of stock, which is £1,052,631 of stock. Because the stock is priced at 95, each £1 buys more than £1 nominal amount of stock – if the price were 100, then £1 would buy £1 nominal amount of stock. As a result, the bank receives 10% of £1.052,631, ie £105,263.10 pa until 2006, when it receives the £1,052,231 from the government, on maturity.

The problem with such stocks is that the price varies with the level of interest rates, falling when rates rise and rising when interest rates fall, as we saw with bills.

Another different type of investment is a trade investment, such as Abbey National's shareholding in DAH Holdings Ltd, which provides private banking services in Hong Kong and the Channel Islands.

Other assets

A large part of these are the premises of the major retail banks. These run into many thousands of properties. Today, all banks also hold an increasing part of their assets in computers and terminals and other equipment.

Liquid assets

These are marked with (L). By no stretch of the imagination can advances, trade investments and premises be considered liquid – they are not easily convertible into cash without delay, undue expense or loss.

Other activities of banks

There are probably over 250 different services, or products as they are often called, available from banks. Here, we have space for only some major activities. Most, apart from foreign exchange business, do not involve the major assets of the banks and hence have been called non-funds based products.

Foreign exchange dealing

These transactions are really buying and selling bank deposits expressed in foreign currencies. Thus, a bank will buy Swiss francs and sell US dollars, placing the francs in its account with a bank in Zurich and paying dollars from its account with a bank in New York to the purchaser's bank in that city. The balances of these accounts will be included with advances because the bank is lending the currency to the two banks with which it has accounts. In fact, most major banks maintain accounts with hundreds of banks overseas – known as nostro accounts – our accounts with you.

If the bank overseas maintains sterling accounts with a bank in London then the balances will appear in the UK bank's balance sheet under deposits. A UK bank will refer to these sterling accounts maintained by these overseas correspondent banks as vostro accounts – your accounts with us.

Although the deposits in sterling and foreign currencies appear in the balance sheet, the actual transactions do not. These can amount to many millions of pounds a day for a bank, when the sterling equivalents are calculated and, for London as a whole, the total can be as high as £90bn a day!

In London, banks deal with each other using a broker who charges a small fee for putting buyer and seller in touch. International deals, say between Barclays in London and Chase Manhattan in New York, are between banks directly, by telephone, telex, fax or computer.

Share registration

This product for company customers has grown rapidly since 1960 and involves maintaining a register (a list, that is) of all shareholders, paying the dividends and altering the register when shares are bought and sold.

Major banks in this market include:

- Lloyds TSB;

- Royal Bank of Scotland, which recently bought NatWest's operations.

Also, Abbey National has recently taken its share register away from Lloyds Bank, and set up its own department, with a view to competing with the other banks.

Global custody

Here, custodian banks hold the securities which investing institutions purchase and sell around the world.

Estate agencies and insurance companies

Some, but not all, banks purchased firms of estate agencies in the late 1980s and have set up their own insurance broking subsidiaries. Estate agencies do not buy and sell houses but merely act for sellers of houses, charging a commission when the house is sold. Insurance brokers merely place business with insurers, who write the policies, receiving a fee from the insurers.

All that appears in the balance sheets of the owning banks is the relatively small amount spent in buying these businesses or any loans which may have been made to enable the businesses to expand.

Executor and trustee business

Executors are people or organizations appointed by a person's will to carry it out exactly as he or she requests and, since the early days of this century, banks have offered this service to people drawing up their wills.

The heyday of this service was in the middle of the 20th century but today many people own little apart from their house and a company pension. The day of the private shareholder has largely gone, although the government has been trying to encourage people to own more shares. Hence, this service has declined, with many specialist executor and trustee branches being closed, or replaced by private banking branches.

Private banking

Aimed at wealthier customers, this entails managing investments on their behalf and providing executor and trustee services for them. It has grown considerably since the late 1980s.

Retail banks

These are banks which have large branch networks and also take an active role in the cheque and credit clearings. They place few restrictions on the minimum size of an account although there are quite high minima on certain accounts. £1 will open a current account, whereas at least £10,000 may be needed for a premium investment account. Most retail banks offer the full range of banking services, but not necessarily through every local branch. As we mentioned in Chapter 1, the largest retail banks also have very important operations in the wholesale markets.

In the mid-1990s the Bank of England considered the following to be retail banks:

Barclays; Midland; Lloyds TSB; National Westminster (including Coutts); Abbey National; Co-operative Bank; Yorkshire Bank; Bank of Scotland; Clydesdale Bank; Royal Bank of Scotland; Girobank; Ulster Bank; Bank of Ireland; Northern Bank.

In June 1995, their total liabilities including capital were £589bn, of which foreign currency deposits were £134bn. Today, the Bank of England no longer publishes separate statistics for types of banks.

The conversions of building societies are one reason why the Bank of England no longer publishes its series of statistics for retail banks and other types of banks. A second reason is that many non-banking subsidiaries are now treated as banks so that the 'population' of banks has been increasing. Again, there have been a number of new entrants to the retail banking market, as we have seen. An additional reason is that many banks now deal in swaps, futures and options to a very large extent, so that these new assets distort any comparisons with earlier statistics. Assets bought under 'sale and repurchase' (termed 'repo') transactions are effectively treated as secured loans, while assets sold under these repo transactions remain on the balance sheets, with a liability to the purchaser recorded under liabilities.

Wholesale banks

These are not retail banks in the Bank of England's classification and have either a limited branch network or deliberately choose to operate only in wholesale money markets. Many will specialize in foreign currency loans, deposits and purchases and sales. The Bank of England classified them into:

- Japanese banks.

- American banks.

- Other overseas banks including consortium banks.

- British merchant banks, which were members of the London Investment Banking Association. This replaced the narrowly-based Accepting Houses Committee, which had 16 members. Merchant banks specialize in trade finance and, more importantly, in advice on company mergers, take-overs etc. Recently, many merchant banks have become known as investment banks. Most are now owned by overseas banks.

- Other British banks.

There was another category, consortium banks, which were banks owned by two or more other banks of which at least one was a foreign bank. However, most foreign banks prefer to have their own operations in London and so consortium banks were then included with other overseas banks because their operations had declined.

Figure 4
Liabilities of All Banks in UK 1994, 1997 and 2001

	1994 £m	1997 £m	2001 £m
Sterling deposits	510,346	907,422	1,238,548
Foreign currency deposits	1,471,513	783,987	1,026,328
CDs and short-term paper issued	131,749	250,886	383,430
Other liabilities	125,503	272,302	394,741
Total	1,551,584	2,456,940	3,488,232

Source: Bank of England.

Girobank Plc

The Girobank is sometimes confused with the National Savings Bank. Since its foundation in 1968, the Girobank has had three names and two owners, so it is not surprising that confusion occurs!

Its first name was the National Giro, being set up under the former Postmaster General to provide a centralized clearing system to compete with the Big Five Banks of that time for the business of ordinary people. Giro means 'circulation' and is a term used in many European countries. All the accounts are kept at Bootle, near Liverpool, and the 21,000 or so post offices are used as sales outlets.

The established retail banks responded by renaming their credit slips 'bank giro credits'. Then, in 1978 the National Giro became the National Girobank. Later, as part of the reorganization of the Post Office, it became the Girobank Plc, with Post Office Counters Ltd (now Post Office Ltd, part of the Consignia group) providing the face-to-face contact with most customers and with the Post Office Corporation as its owner. To add to the confusion, many post offices still have plaques in their walls inscribed National Girobank.

By the late 1980s, Girobank's computers needed complete replacement and, in view of government policy to privatize where possible and to cut back on expenditure, it was decided to offer Girobank for sale. The eventual purchaser was the Alliance & Leicester Building Society (now Alliance & Leicester plc).

Girobank now has a substantial customer base, with a major share of the market for moving cash for large multiple stores and supermarkets, although it transferred its VISA credit card business to the Co-operative Bank.

National Savings Bank

Apart from using Post Office Counters Ltd (now Post Office Ltd), this has little in common with Girobank Plc, which had become something of a political football.

Founded by Gladstone in 1861 as the Post Office Savings Bank, and renamed National Savings Bank in 1971, this is far from being a political football. It provides savings facilities for small savers via the post office network and via its main office in Glasgow.

Strictly, it is not a bank, because it does not lend to anybody apart from its owner – the government. However, it can provide effective competition for banks in certain markets, because all interest is paid without income tax being deducted at source. The retail markets where it has a competitive edge over banks and building societies are those where people do not pay income tax – young people, pensioners and some married women.

Its deposits have totalled around £10bn for some years. Its rates of interest are determined largely by the long-term rate of interest which the Government has to pay when it issues gilt-edged loan stock rather than by what retail banks are paying on savings and deposit accounts. Because this long-term rate was falling in 2001, the National Savings Bank often received unfavourable media comment for paying what financial journalists regarded as poor rates of interest.

Building societies

These are mutual organizations governed by special Acts of Parliament which strictly limit their functions. Each society is governed by its own rules but these rules can only authorize it to do things permitted by Act of Parliament. The current Acts are the Building Societies Act 1986 which greatly extended the range of societies' activities and allowed each one to raise a minimum of 50% of its deposits through the wholesale markets mentioned earlier in this chapter, and the Building Societies Act 1997 which gave societies the option (if their members agreed) of undertaking more activities and which also made their directors more accountable to their members. The 1983 Finance Act had allowed them to issue CDs and the 1989 Finance Act allowed them to issue CP.

The building society movement began 200 years ago but its real growth was in the 20th century and associated with the decline of homes rented from private owners, which were very common about 100 years ago, in favour of owner-occupation, which accounts for about 66% of all homes today. There are now fewer than 80 societies. Obviously, many investors have accounts with more than one society, so there is a great deal of double counting of investors. The Halifax, with deposits of over £75bn, was the world's largest building society and the Abbey National was the second largest before they became banks. The Nationwide is now the world's largest building society.

Apart from satisfying people's need to own their homes, the

societies' success has been achieved by their willingness and ability to open for longer hours than banks and to pay very attractive rates of interest on all money invested with them. Banks began to compete seriously with the societies in 1980 with the competition taking the following forms:

- Banks offering home loans in 1981.

- Building societies issuing CDs in 1983, to tap the wholesale markets used by the banks.

- Banks offering better interest rates on their deposit and savings accounts.

- Societies seeking parliamentary powers to operate current accounts, given in the 1986 Act, along with many other powers, including conversion to a bank. Banks responded in 1989 by offering current accounts that pay interest on credit balances.

- In 1989 Abbey National became a bank, a move followed by the Alliance & Leicester's purchase of Girobank. In 1995, Lloyds Bank bought the Cheltenham & Gloucester Building Society; in 1996 Abbey National bought the National & Provincial Building Society; in 1997 the Halifax became a bank, along with the other societies previously mentioned.

At present, there is hardly any competition between banks and building societies for commercial customers, but this is likely to develop within the next five years if societies take advantage of new powers offered to them to provide banking services for small firms. However, a regional building society in East Anglia (the Norwich and Peterborough) has a current account for small businesses including limited companies. There are two restrictions: no coins are accepted as deposits and the account must stay in credit.

Societies were regulated by the Building Societies Commission, which was linked to the Registrar of Friendly Societies and which reported to the Treasury. Banks were regulated by the Bank of England, which also reported to the Treasury. Both are now regulated by the Financial Services Authority.

Banks and building societies compete fiercely in the following personal markets:

- Current accounts;

- Deposit and savings accounts;

- Home loans.

- Travel facilities – traveller's cheques, foreign currency;

- Personal loans;

- Insurance;

- Individual Savings Accounts;

- Credit cards.

They compete less intensively in the market for business customers. Indeed, some observers refer to the converted societies as 'mortgage banks'.

Insurance

Whereas banks are largely companies and building societies are mutual organizations, insurance companies can be either. The largest mutual insurer is Standard Life, while CGNU (shortly to become Aviva and using the Norwich Union brand now) and Royal Sun Alliance are leading insurance companies (with their shares quoted on the stock exchange). Just as building societies have been 'demutualizing', so have some of the mutuals in insurance. Scottish Widows is one, having been taken over by Lloyds TSB Bank at the end of the 1990s, although the brand has been preserved.

The insurance industry is divided into different kinds of insurance. The oldest is marine insurance – 'for those in peril on the sea' – and the insurance covered the hulls of ships as well as their cargoes. The next oldest is fire insurance, probably prompted by the Great Fire of London in 1666. In the next century, the development of mortality tables, enabling forecasts to be made of life expectancy, facilitated the growth of life insurance (or, to give it a more exact name, life assurance). Insurance provides cover in case of uncertain trouble (a possible fire or shipwreck), but death is certain – what is uncertain is the date of our death. Hence, the term is life assurance rather than insurance.

In the 19th century, insurance moved into industrial activities with boiler insurance (against the risk of explosions). In the 20th century, motor and aviation insurance developed and, later, travel insurance.

Also in the last (twentieth) century, some types of insurance became legally obligatory – eg motor insurance and employers' liability insurance. Moreover, in law, insurance contracts are of a special kind – contracts of the utmost good faith (both parties must disclose every material fact to each other). Thirdly, there must be an 'insurable interest' in a policy, otherwise it becomes a wager.

By now, readers will be asking: 'Where do banks and building societies fit in?' The answer is that they lend money against the security of mortgages over property, which needs to be adequately insured against fire, flood or other damage. If not, and the worst happens, the property may not be worth as much as the loan. So, banks and building societies have an interest in ensuring that there is adequate insurance cover. And, of course, lenders have an insurable interest in the lives of their debtors.

A century ago, banks allowed their branch managers to collect the commission from selling insurance policies and to keep it as a financial 'perk'. Later, the banks took the premium income into their own profits and moved into some, but not all, of the various types of insurance.

As well as being divided into different areas – fire, marine, motor, aviation, life – the business of insurance is also divided into selling policies and writing policies. Policies are sold, as a rule, by insurance brokers but the risks of paying claims and determining premiums are carried by those who 'write' (to use a technical term) the policies. So as to minimize the risks, the task of 'writing' policies is shared by a team of 'underwriters' who agree to take part of the risk in return for receiving part of the premiums. The most famous underwriters are the Lloyd's Names, who underwrite the policies issued by Lloyd's members.

To return to banking. Banks (and building societies) have been selective in the areas of insurance they have entered. First, they have moved into broking rather than underwriting. Secondly, they have avoided aviation and marine, preferring life, household (structural and contents) and travel insurance (which fits into their foreign notes and coins business). It is very rare for a bank to be involved in underwriting insurance policies. In a similar way, insurance companies and mutuals have preferred personal banking rather than business banking when they entered the banking markets towards the end of the 20th century.

Summary

- Commercial banks have the following main assets, arranged in order of liquidity: notes and coin, balances with the Bank of England, inter-bank loans, bills, advances, investments, premises and computers.

- Foreign currency assets are greater than sterling assets.

- These assets are funded by sight deposits, time deposits, CDs, repos and capital.

- Non-funds based products include: share registration, investment management, estate agencies, insurance broking companies, and executor and trustee services.

- Retail banks have a large branch network and are members of the clearing systems. Most are also active in the wholesale market.

- Wholesale banks do not usually have branches and clear their cheques through a retail bank.

- Girobank is a unique retail bank, operating over post office counters, and owned by a former building society.

- The National Savings Bank is not a commercial bank, although it does compete with the commercial banks for small savings. It operates through the Post Office.

- Building societies are, as a result of great expansion this century, virtually the same as banks to many people. Although providing many similar services to banks, they were regulated under different systems, but now have the same regulator.

- Insurance comprises several fields – marine, fire, motor, life are some examples. Firms can be brokers or writers.

[Answer to question earlier in chapter: about £9,900 if the bill has three months to maturity]

Further Reading – Chapter 5

Anderton B (Ed), (1995) *Current Issues in Financial Services,* Chapters 9-10. MacMillan. ISBN 0 333 56799 4

Llewellyn D, (1997) *Reflections on the Mutuality v Conversion Debate,* Building Societies Association. See also other papers published by the BSA.

Annual Reports of The Banking Ombudsman Scheme, The Office of the Banking Ombudsman. Financial Ombudsman Service (when published).

Holyoake J and Weipers, B (2002) *Insurance. 5th edition.* CIB Publishing. ISBN 0-85297-675-5.

6 The City of London and the Bank of England

Objectives

After studying this chapter you should be able to:

- [ ] Explain why the Stock Exchange is important.

- [ ] Name two different types of securities bought and sold on the stock exchange.

- [ ] Describe the role played by life assurance companies and pension funds.

- [ ] Outline the role of the London International Financial Futures and Options Exchange (LIFFE).

- [ ] Discuss the nature of financial intermediation and the differences between banks and building societies and the other financial intermediaries.

- [ ] Explain what was meant by Big Bang.

- [ ] Outline how prudential regulation and customer protection is provided for banks, building societies and the other financial intermediaries.

- [ ] State the functions and explain the role of the Bank of England.

Introduction

The term 'City' is used to describe all the financial and other markets operating in an area in London of about half a mile radius of the Bank of England (sometimes known as the square mile). These include the wholesale money markets, the foreign exchange market, the Stock Exchange, the London International Financial Futures and Options Exchange, the Baltic Exchange and a range of commodity markets. Several investment banks and firms have moved about two miles eastwards into Docklands – seen by some observers as a threat to the old City.

The discount market comprised the Bank of England, discount houses and some hundreds of commercial banks. It acted as a 'cushion' between the government and the banking system and it was where the Bank of England sought to implement the government's interest-rate policy. The Bank of England now signals changes in the short-term interest rates of banks and building societies by changing its repo interest rate.

The London Stock Exchange

Its correct title is the International Stock Exchange and it underwent considerable changes in the mid 1980s, culminating in 'Big Bang' on 27 October 1986. Prior to that, its member firms were of two kinds:

- Brokers, with their incomes from commissions charged to investors, and acting purely as agents.

- Jobbers, who owned the stocks and shares, making an income from profits arising from the margins between their buying and selling prices to the brokers.

Big Bang comprised a series of changes, agreed with the government, to make the exchange more competitive with the New York and Tokyo exchanges, which are its major competitors.

Until Big Bang, the rule was single capacity – a firm could be either a broker or a jobber but not both. Also, until Big Bang, commissions charged were not negotiable and this lack of competition caused international business to move to New York and Tokyo.

Big Bang also made the following changes:

- Minimum commissions were abolished.

- Firms could be brokers and jobbers, known as market makers, although many smaller ones preferred to remain as brokers.

- Banks, both foreign and UK, could own firms of brokers and market makers.

- Trading went from the 'floor', where dealers met each other, to screens and telephones.

The main market of the London Stock Exchange is divided into two:

- Gilt-edged (gilts) and other fixed-interest stocks;

- Equities.

Gilts

Gilts are, as we saw in the previous chapter, fixed-interest marketable securities issued by the government. On 31 March 1997 there were £290bn of gilts outstanding, grouped as follows:

Figure 5
Gilts Outstanding as at 31 March 2000

	£bn
Short-dated, repayable by the government within 5 years	95.2
Medium-dated, repayable between 5-15 years	116.9
Long-dated, repayable in over 15 years' time	75.4
Undated, no repayment date	3.2
Total	290.6

This total has risen from £122bn in 1991.

Total transactions in British government securities in 2000 were £1,595bn, or £1.6 trillion. This is the latest year for which complete data are available.

The firms involved in the gilt-edged market are of three types:

- Gilt-edged market makers, committed to buying and selling the stocks;

- Stock Exchange money brokers, who lend stocks to market makers and can also lend market makers money at competitive rates against the security of the stocks owned by the market makers.

- Inter-dealer brokers, who enable market makers to deal with each other with complete anonymity.

The Bank of England provides a central gilts office, with computerized records, which now handles most gilt-edged transactions. Settlement of all deals takes place the next business day.

Equities

Equities are the shares of limited companies, so called because they have claims on the companies' assets only after all creditors have been paid. So, these are shares of 'what is left'. (We shall meet the term again when we consider home loans – the equity in a house is what it is worth after the mortgage(s) has/have been repaid.)

Just as there are gilt-edged market makers, so there are equity market makers but they need not be the same firms.

In 2000, transactions in UK and Irish equities totalled £1,795bn.

Transactions are settled, ie, paid for, after five working days. Known as T-5, it is hoped to reduce this period to three days soon. However, for small investors and their transactions the settlement period is ten working days.

The Stock Exchange provides a primary market for the government and companies to borrow money, and for companies to issue shares, often for cash. It also is a secondary market where investors can sell and buy stocks and shares – a market in 'second-hand' or existing stocks and shares.

The major investors in the Stock Exchange are not rich individuals but life assurance companies and pension funds. Together, they are known as the institutions and they are very important. At the end of 2000, pension funds and insurance companies had total financial assets of £1,612bn, with £197bn invested in gilts, £691bn in UK equities and £234bn in the equities of overseas companies.

London International Financial Futures and Options Exchange (LIFFE)

LIFFE was founded in 1982 and provides opportunities to buy and sell both futures and options in currencies, gilts and comparable foreign securities. It became the third largest such market in the world, after the two in Chicago, where futures began last century (in agricultural products).

However, it has faced severe competition from the French derivatives exchange (MATIF) and from direct deals between international banks in what are termed OTC (over-the-counter) transactions.

A future is a commitment, ie an obligation, to buy or sell currency or a security at a certain future date. The firm owning the commitment can always sell it before the date arrives, if it wishes to do so.

An option is a right, but not an obligation, to buy or sell currency, etc up to a certain date.

Futures and options are given a technical name – derivatives – because their prices are derived from the prices of the instruments and currencies on the ordinary (cash) markets.

Other markets

The Baltic Exchange specializes in the chartering of ships and aircraft. In addition, there are a number of City markets dealing in commodities, such as the London Metal Exchange, and the 'soft' commodities such as cocoa and coffee.

Lloyd's

This is nothing to do with Lloyds Bank but is an insurance organization, whose individual members (known as Names) accept unlimited liability for the losses sustained on the insurance business they accept. Lloyd's operates worldwide, insuring anything from a commercial satellite or a ship to a bank clerk's motor car. The business is brought to Lloyd's by brokers who charge commission for their services to the people seeking insurance. The risks to be insured are accepted by underwriters who act for syndicates of members. Obviously, members should belong to as many different syndicates as possible, to spread their own risks. Members have been mainly rich individuals with at least £250,000, excluding their house. However, more limited companies are being formed to underwrite insurance at Lloyds, and soon Names could become history.

Financial intermediation

Banks, building societies, pension funds and life assurance companies are the four largest financial intermediaries linking ultimate borrowers with ultimate borrowers with ultimate lenders. The ultimate borrowers are those to whom banks and building societies lend, and those companies and the UK government, in whom the pension funds and insurance companies invest. The ultimate lenders are the depositors with the banks and building societies, the workers in the pension funds and the policyholders with the life assurance companies.

There are several advantages of financial intermediation. It enables:

- Sums of money to be 'parcelled up' – aggregated – to lend to large borrowers such as ICI, or to be 'unbundled' when banks and building societies borrow on the wholesale markets and lend to house buyers.

- The length of a transaction to be varied, eg depositors can withdraw their funds from a building society which lends for up to 25 years for home loans. (It would be very embarrassing if depositors had to get their money direct from the borrower buying the house!)

- The intermediary – the bank, etc – to bear any risk of loss. There are also schemes to protect the small original lenders (see below).

- The intermediary to reduce the time and effort needed if the borrower were to get in touch directly with the lender.

Banks have been regarded as a special type of intermediary because only their liabilities – notes and deposits – are accepted as money. But, as we have seen, the liabilities of building societies are also accepted as money, so they must now be classed as 'bank financial intermediaries'. That leaves pension funds and insurance companies as the major non-bank financial intermediaries (NBFIs).

A more up-to-date classification is into deposit-taking and investing financial intermediaries or into Monetary Financial Institutions (banks and building societies) and Other Financial Institutions.

Other, smaller NBFIs are unit trusts, investment trusts and finance houses. A relatively new type of NBFI is the 'centralized mortgage institution', such as the Mortgage Corporation or the Home Loans Corporation. These borrow on the wholesale money market or on the Stock Exchange and lend on to home-owners and mortgagors.

Credit Unions are a very small type of NBFI, comprising 'savings clubs' for people united by common links such as religion, living in the same area or working for the same employer. They are common in Canada and Ireland, but still rare in Great Britain. Their regulator is the Registrar of Friendly Societies.

Financial regulation

Until recently there were broadly three main regulators:

- The Bank of England, regulating banks, the wholesale money markets, the foreign exchange market, and the gilt-edged market. For bank regulation, the statute is the Banking Act 1987.

- The Building Societies Commission, controlling building societies under the Building Societies Act 1986 and 1997.

- The Securities and Investment Board (SIB) controlling the rest of the financial activities, and set up under the Financial Services Act 1986. Under the Financial Services and Markets Act 2000 its role was undertaken by the Financial Services Authority (FSA), which has also taken over the supervision of banks and building societies.

The SIB worked mainly through three self-regulatory organizations (SROs) whose work is undertaken by the FSA. The initials may still appear on old stationery used by financial service firms.

IMRO
This stood for Investment Management Regulatory Organization. It comprised fund managers who manage pension funds etc, and was the SRO to which the major banks belonged, because fund management is not covered under the Banking Act 1987.

Personal Investment Authority
This SRO was based on the personal market rather than the type of services sold. It covered life assurance, unit trusts and personal pensions, whether sold by tied agents or independent advisers. Its members included the financial services subsidiaries of retail banks and building societies, as well as many of the banks and building societies themselves and independent financial advisers.

SFA
This stood for the Securities and Futures Authority, which dealt with all Stock Exchange and futures transactions, so that it regulated LIFFE and the commodity markets' transactions in futures and options.

In addition, some chartered accountants and solicitors are able to give advice on investments by virtue of the regulation applied by their governing bodies – the Institute of Chartered Accountants and the Law Society respectively.

Consumer protection

As well as the three SROs and the SIB, there were three important Ombudsmen – grievance men – for banks, building societies and insurance. The Insurance Ombudsman's office was the oldest and that of the Banking Ombudsman was modelled on it. These two were voluntary but the Building Societies Ombudsman was statutory, being created by the Building Societies Act 1986. They, and a number of others, have been combined into a new Financial Ombudsman Service.

The alternative to an ombudsman is a code of practice, as established for estate agents and finance houses.

The Banking Ombudsman began work in early 1986. He was a lawyer, independent of the banks and responsible to an independent council. His work is now undertaken by the Financial Ombudsman Service (FOS), whose functions are to:

- Work, within the existing law, as an impartial adjudicator in unresolved personal disputes between individuals, and financial firms which must accept its decisions but complainants dissatisfied with its decisions still have the right to begin legal proceedings against the bank involved. However, it will not investigate complaints where legal proceedings have already begun.

Matters covered by the FOS include banking services, credit cards issued by banks and building societies (ie, not those issued directly by stores and other non-financial businesses), insurance policies, pensions, mortgages, stocks and shares and unit trusts.

Protection funds

The Banking Act 1987 specified the protection afforded to personal depositors in banks. 90% of their deposits, subject to a maximum protected sterling deposit of £20,000, were protected if the bank should get into difficulties. In practice, this meant that the maximum amount depositors could get back from a bank was £18,000. Foreign currency deposits were excluded.

The Building Societies Investment Protection Fund gave similar protection.

There is also a Policy Holders Protection Fund for the insurance industry.

These three funds have been absorbed into a new Financial Services Compensation Scheme. The 90% of the value of an insurance policy under the Policyholders Protection Act continues, as do the amounts available if an investment firm becomes insolvent. These are 100% of the first £30,000 and 90% of the next £20,000 (making £48,000 as the maximum).

However, the limits and the method of calculation for bank and building society failures have been changed. Before N2 (1 December 2001) everybody with a deposit of £20,000 or less lost 10%, with maximum compensation of £18,000. The reasoning behind this method of calculation was to avoid 'moral hazard' (depositors ignoring risk because they would get all their money back).

The new system provides for

    100% return of the first £2,000 deposited
plus   90% return of the next £33,000.

This gives £31,700 (£2,000 + £29,700) for the first £35,000 deposited.

The Banking Code

This is a code of practice drawn up by the:

- British Bankers' Association (BBA)

- Building Societies Association (BSA)

- Association for Payment Clearing Services (APACS) which we discuss later and which operates the clearings.

It was launched in 1992, revised in 1994 and again in 1997 and 2001. It is a voluntary code setting out the standards of good banking practice to be observed by banks, building societies and plastic card issuers in their relations with personal customers in the UK.

Mortgages are covered by a separate code.

The Bank of England

The Bank is now much smaller than it was at the beginning of the 1990s. Its functions are still numerous, however, and can be grouped under three headings:

A. Monetary Stability

Here, the emphasis is on achieving monetary stability – of prices, interest rates and exchange rates. This is a continental European definition of monetary stability: an Anglicised version might be to achieve the inflation target remitted to the Bank by the Chancellor of the Exchequer. This might, of course, entail some element of instability in interest rates and, possibly, in exchange rates.

This section of the Bank is concerned with:

1. Producing the quarterly Inflation Report and the Quarterly Bulletin. The Inflation Report is, from its name, focused upon the outlook for inflation and provides an analytical benchmark for the decision-taking of the Monetary Policy Committee. The Quarterly Bulletin is more broadly based and comprises surveys of monetary policy developments in the markets of the world and, of course, in the UK.

   It also publishes articles on specialist topics, but written in language for the general reader, from the Bank's staff as well as speeches by the Governor and other directors.

2. Economic and monetary analysis in support of the work of the Monetary Policy Committee in achieving the Government's inflation target, currently 2.5% pa for RPIX in approximately two years' time. RPIX is the 'buzz-word' for the ordinary retail prices index excluding payments of mortgage interest and was mentioned in Chapter 3 earlier in this book.

3. Regional agencies (once known as branches) monitoring the state of trade and industry in various parts of the UK.

4. The compilation and publication of Monetary and Financial Statistics.

B. Financial Stability

The Bank of England is no longer concerned with regulating individual commercial banks – a function which went to the Financial Services Authority on 1 June 1998. Instead, it is now concerned with the smooth operation of the various financial markets and, in particular, with ensuring that there is no systemic failure of them – what a layman might describe as a 'financial meltdown' and what the Governor has likened to an avalanche. Some quarter of a century ago, this possible systemic failure was referred to as the 'domino effect' – the collapse of one institution (say, for example from more recent events, Barings or BCCI) triggering the collapse of other banks which had entered into deals with the failed institution or because investors/depositors were stampeding into withdrawing funds or refusing to deal with other institutions. To elaborate upon the Governor's analogy, the Bank no longer checks the climbers and their equipment but it does keep a weather eye open for an avalanche which could overcome them all, irrespective of their personal qualities and gear.

Students should be advised not to confuse 'systematic risk' with 'systemic risk'. The former includes risk which is generalized in its effect, and which involves most participants in the markets, while the latter can result in the breakdown of the whole of the market system. The millennium bug was a topical example of a possible systemic risk, although it was a risk which is technical rather than related to the confidence of market participants.

The work of this section covers:

1. Markets and trading systems. This division supports the Bank's operations in support of monetary policy, by providing 'back office' facilities in the form of the Central Gilts Office (CGO) and the Central Moneymarkets Office (CMO).

2. Financial intermediaries, which are not insurance salesmen (a modern connotation) but what were once called non-banking financial intermediaries, such as pension funds, life assurance companies, unit trusts and investment trusts.

3. Regulatory policy. This division oversaw the transfer of the responsibility for banking supervision to the FSA, but it

continues to provide briefings and research on broader regulatory issues, including regulatory incentives, value at risk (VAR) modelling and the measurement of credit risk. It has also begun to represent the Bank on several international supervisory committees, including the Basle Supervisors' Committee.

There is a possibility of an overlap between the work of this section and that of the Financial Services Authority and the Treasury (which was responsible for regulating general insurance companies and Lloyd's of London). Consequently, there is a Memorandum of Understanding between the Bank, FSA and Treasury, while the Bank's Deputy Governor (financial stability) is a member of the FSA Board and the Chairman of the FSA is a member of the Court (ie, the board) of the Bank of England. In addition, there is a Standing Committee of all three parties to the Memorandum, meeting monthly and, if needs be, at very short notice.

4.   Payment and Settlement Policy. Recently, this section has been concerned with preparations for EMU and the negotiations over the TARGET (wait for it! – Trans-European Automated Real-time Gross settlement Express Transfer system) which some EU central bankers and politicians wish to be unavailable to central banks not in the 'first wave' of eleven members of the single currency area. Other aspects of this section's work have included the minimization of risks in the settlement of foreign exchange and derivative transactions, a proposed merger of the CGO (gilts settlements) and CREST (equity settlements) and preparations for the year 2000.

C. Operations in financial markets
The above overlaps both monetary and financial stability

1.   In the gilt-edged and money markets, where the Bank deals on behalf of customers other than the UK Government, which now deals through the Treasury.

2.   In banking, where the Bank still acts for the UK government, its largest customer.

3.   In the foreign exchange market, where the Bank still acts for the UK government, its largest customer.

4.   In its stock registration services, primarily for gilt-edged stock but also for stocks issued by other borrowers, such as some local authorities.

D. Printing

Unlike some continental European central banks, the Bank still prints its banknotes.

The Bank's latest Annual Report summarizes the Bank's core purposes as to:

1.   Maintaining the integrity and value of the currency.

2.   Maintaining the stability of the financial system, both domestic and international.

3.   Seeking to ensure the effectiveness of the UK's financial services, so as to enhance the international competitiveness of the City of London and other UK financial centres.

Summary

- It is in its day-to-day operations in the repo market that the Bank of England seeks to influence the level of interest rates, to implement the government's monetary policy.

- The Stock Exchange is dominated by pension funds and life assurance companies, investing in British government securities (gilts) and the ordinary shares of companies (equities).

- Big Bang (27 October 1986) abolished minimum commissions, the distinction between jobbers and brokers and the ban on banks owning member firms.

- Financial intermediaries put ultimate borrowers in touch with ultimate lenders. The major intermediaries are banks, building societies, pension funds and life assurance companies.

- The Bank of England has many functions. These can be grouped into: monetary stability, financial stability and operations in financial markets, and printing.

- Financial regulation is governed by four Acts of Parliament: Building Societies Acts 1986 and 1987, Financial Services Act 1986 and the Banking Act 1987. However, changes are now occurring in advance of a new Financial Services and Markets Act.

Further Reading – Chapter 6

Anderton B (Ed), (1995) *Current Issues in Financial Services,* Chapters 2, 3 and 11. MacMillan. ISBN 0 333 56799 4.
Annual Reports and Accounts of the Bank of England.
Annual Banking Act Reports of the Bank of England.
Bank of England Quarterly Bulletin. ISBN 0005 5166.

7 The banker-customer relationship

Objectives

After studying this chapter you should be able to:

- [ ] State the legal definitions of a bank and a customer.

- [ ] Describe the various legal principles underlying the banker-customer relationship.

- [ ] State the rights and duties of banker and customer.

- [ ] Outline the broad recommendations of the Jack Committee regarding this relationship, especially the bank's duty of secrecy.

- [ ] Outline the main provisions of the Banking Code.

Introduction

Here, we are concerned with law, which is of two kinds – statutes (Acts of Parliament) and case law, decided by the courts. The importance of a case depends mainly on the status of the court in which the case was heard. The senior court is the House of Lords, whose decisions are binding on all courts in the UK. Next comes the Court of Appeal, which is bound by the Lords' decisions but which can bind the lower courts such as the High Court. Occasionally, court or judge can avoid following the decision in a case by carefully distinguishing it, ie spelling out the reasons why the facts in the new case differ from those in the older case. Acts of Parliament can overrule any decision of any English Court.

Thus, in our first section, we plunge into statute law and case law to establish the legal definition of a bank.

What is a bank?

Until 1966 there were no clear rules. One or two Acts of Parliament defined a bank but only for purposes of that particular Act. For instance, there was a definition in the Income Tax Acts and another for the Bills of Exchange Act 1882 and yet another for the Building Societies Act 1962.

But in the case of United Dominions *Trust v Kirkwood* (1966), the Court of Appeal had to decide whether UDT was a bank. UDT sued Kirkwood for a debt. His defence was that UDT was a moneylender and that, because the Moneylenders Act 1900 required all moneylenders to be registered before they could sue for their debts, UDT could not sue him. UDT had not registered as a moneylender. The court found that UDT was not a moneylender but a bank and therefore was not required to register under the Act. The Court of Appeal stated four reasons for deciding that UDT was as a bank. It:

- Kept accounts which were debited and credited.

- Credited money from customers, in the form of cheques and cash.

- Debited its customers' accounts with cheques and standing orders.

- Was regarded as a bank by the financial community.

These four characteristics are now regarded as the 'tests' for a bank.

In 1979 the Banking Act gave a more precise definition, which has been changed by the Banking Act of 1987. The latter Act stipulates that a bank must be a deposit-taking institution authorized under that Act and one which has net assets (paid-up capital and reserves) of not less than ECU 5m. If the net assets are less than this (about £4m), then the firm is only an authorized deposit-taking institution and not permitted to use the word 'bank' in its name. Every authorized deposit-taking institution must have:

- Fit and proper people as directors.

- At least two people effectively directing its business.

- Its business conducted in a prudent manner, ie:
  - net assets which are at least ECU 1m and adequate in relation to the size and risks of the business;
  - adequate liquidity;
  - adequate depreciation, and bad debt provision;
  - maintain adequate records.

The situation now is that the courts will look to the 1987 Act and to the list of authorized banks which the Bank of England publishes and also to the rules outlined in Kirkwood's Case. There are still plenty of 'grey areas'. For instance, would the courts regard a deposit-taking institution with only £2m of net assets as a bank even though it could not use 'bank' in its name?

Since 1998 The Financial Services Authority has been the banks' regulator. The FSA promises to unify the different regulatory regimes covering the separate parts of the Financial Services industry. It will use a risk-based approach to regulation.

Who is a customer?

This is a most important question on which depends two things:

- Customers are owed some ten duties by their banks but banks do not owe these duties to non-customers.

- A bank obtains statutory protection if it acts for a customer, eg under the Cheques Act 1957, but not if it acts for a non-customer.

A customer can be defined as a person or organization with a current or similar account with a bank. The length of time of the relationship is not important because the relationship starts when the application to open the account is accepted.

An example of a person using a bank but who is not a customer would be someone merely cashing a cheque at that bank, with a cheque card issued by another bank. Borderline cases (or 'grey areas') might be individuals without current accounts but with fixed-term deposits with the wholesale money market divisions or treasurers' departments of banks. People holding accounts with the Access or Visa Departments of banks are not regarded as customers – credit card departments term such people as cardholders and not customers.

However, a bank can, in specific circumstances, owe duties to people who are not its customers. For example, in *Woods v Martins Bank* (1959) W, on going to open an account with the bank, asked the manager for investment advice. The manager advised W to invest in one of his branch's customers, a private limited company which was already in financial difficulties. Later the company went into liquidation and W lost money. W sued the bank. The court held that the bank was liable to be as careful in its dealings with W as if he had actually been a customer. (Giving investment advice is now covered by the Financial Services and Markets Act 2000 that came into force on 1 December 2001).

Banker-customer relationship

Debtor and creditor

The main relationship is that of debtor and creditor. A customer who has deposited money (the creditor) is owed money by the bank (the debtor). A customer (the debtor) who has borrowed money from the bank owes money to the bank (the creditor).

In *Foley v Hill* (1848), the customer argued that the relationship was different – the bank was a trustee of the money which he had deposited and that he therefore had a right to share in the profits (trustees have special duties to the people for whom they act as trustees). It was held that there was no element of trusteeship, the relationship being merely that of debtor and creditor.

However, there is something unusual about this relationship because the general practice is that the debtor has a duty to seek out and repay his creditors. This does not apply to banks who are debtors, ie have had money deposited with them. Think about it for a minute – banks could not continue in business if they had to write to every customer with a current account in credit every January, asking every one of them if they would like their money back!

In *Joachimson v Swiss Bank Corporation* (1921) J was unable to obtain his assets during World War I, and sued the bank afterwards for the return of his money. The Court of Appeal highlighted the need for a customer to demand repayment of his or her money before the bank would have a duty to repay. Until the demand, the money was owned by the bank.

Remember, please, that this unusual aspect of the relationship does not apply if the bank is the creditor (the lender). Unless the borrowing is taken by way of a loan account, the borrowing customer should seek out his creditor (the bank).

This case also went on to describe other aspects of the debtor-creditor relationship where the bank is debtor. Thus, just as it is impractical to expect banks to seek out their depositors (creditors) so it is unreasonable for customers to demand payment at any branch or at any time. Demand must be made by the customer:

- In writing.

- During bank hours.

- At the branch where the account is maintained or at a mutually agreed branch.

On its part, the bank must give reasonable notice of the closure of an account in credit.

Principal and agent

When the customer writes a cheque, he or she is the principal, instructing the bank, as the agent, to pay a certain amount of money to a third party (the payee of the cheque).

When the customer buys stocks and shares, or foreign currency/traveller's cheques, this is another example of this legal relationship. This relationship – principal and agent – is becoming more important as banks sell more 'non-funds based products', ie not involving the debtor-creditor relationship which is linked to loans and deposits.

Bailor and bailee

These two terms refer to the contract of bailment, which arises when property is lodged by the bailor with the bailee for specific purpose, eg repair of a motor car or the cleaning of a suit or dress. In banking, the deposit of deeds or securities for safe custody at a branch is an example of bailment. The customer is the bailor, the bank is the bailee.

A paid bailee, known as a bailee for reward, owes a greater degree of care to the bailor than does an unpaid, or gratuitous bailee. The paid bailee must exercise the greatest degree of care, that which people reasonably expect from a person in that type of business. The duty of an unpaid bailee is to care for the property in the same way as a reasonably prudent and careful person would look after his or her own property of a similar type.

Because banks look after their own property exceedingly carefully, it is generally regarded that the distinction between the two types of bailees is not that significant where the banks are concerned.

Mortgagor/mortgagee

Here the mortgagor (customer) has mortgaged his or her property to the bank (mortgagee) as security for a loan or overdraft. The law gives each party certain rights and duties. The property mortgaged is usually land (houses) but can be stocks and shares. Strictly, life assurance policies are not mortgaged but assigned.

A special or fiduciary element

As we saw in connection with the note issue, fiduciary comes from the Latin word *fides*, meaning faith, and the principle requires that the utmost care must be exercised when a bank deals with its customers.

The leading case is *Lloyds v Bundy* (1975), decided by the Court of Appeal. B was an elderly, long-standing customer, with little business competence, relying on the bank for advice. He guaranteed his son's overdraft (with the same branch), executing further guarantees as the debt rose, all supported by mortgages over his farmhouse. A new assistant manager visited the farm, telling B that unless he signed a further guarantee (which the official had in his pocket) the bank would call in his son's borrowing. B signed but some months later the son was made bankrupt and the bank tried to enforce the guarantee and charge, bringing an action for possession of the farmhouse. B sought to set aside the guarantee and charge, maintaining that the bank had exercised undue influence to get it in the first place. The Court held that the bank had to disprove undue influence and that, in the special circumstances, ie the total reliance by B on the bank, it had not done so.

A bank's duties to its customers

1. To honour its customer's cheques to the credit balance on the account or to the agreed overdraft limit, provided:

    a) the cheques are properly drawn and there is not a stop on them;

    b) there are no legal bars to prevent funds being paid to third parties, such as bankruptcy orders or orders of court (see *Whitehead v NatWest Bank,* 1982).

2. To maintain strict secrecy about customers' affairs, subject to certain exceptions (see below).

3. To follow its usual course of business and to be consistent.

4. To give reasonable notice to a customer when closing an account in credit. In *Prosperity Ltd v Lloyds Bank* (1923), P was selling insurance and had printed and distributed prospectuses stating (correctly) that the bank had agreed to accept applications. The scheme was heavily criticized in the press and the bank then wished to close the account and minimize the bad publicity. It gave P one month to close the account, which was in credit. P sued for breach of contract. The bank was held to be in breach of contact because one month's notice was insufficient, given the complex

arrangements made with it for the receipt of applications.

5. To provide a statement of account within a reasonable time and a statement of the balance on request.

    Moreover the bank must keep accurate records. If it wrongly advises a customer of a credit to his or her account then the customer can retain the excess credit if:

    a) the bank misrepresented the account to the customer;

    b) the customer was misled by the inaccurate information and used the funds as a result; and

    c) the customer's position had changed, so that it would be unfair for the customer to repay the money.

    United Overseas Bank v Jiwani (1976) is a good example of these rules. J's account was credited with US$11,000 by telex: whereupon he spent the proceeds of the credit as part payment for a hotel. Later, the bank received a confirmation of the telex message and mistakenly advised J of a further credit of US$11,000, which he again spent. The bank sued J for the return of the second credit. It was held that, while the first two rules applied – the bank had misrepresented the account to the customer, who was misled by this into using the funds as a result of the misrepresentation – the third rule did not. Because J had other funds which he could have used to finance the second transaction, it would therefore be fair for J to repay the money.

6. To receive a customer's money and cheques for collection and to credit his account with them.

7. To repay credit balances on a current account on demand but only:

    a) at the customer's written request;

    b) during banking hours; and

    c) at the branch where the account is maintained or at another mutually agreed branch.

These principles were stated in Joachimson's Case and relate to current accounts.

8. To advise the customer immediately if and when forgery is brought to the Bank's attention. In *Brown v Westminster Bank* (1964), over 100 forged cheques had been paid by the bank but on several occasions the bank had queried the cheques with the customer, who had told it that the signatures were genuine. In fact, the cheques had been forged by B's wife. When she died, B sued the Bank for negligence in paying forged cheques. It was held that, having maintained that the cheques were not forgeries, B could not now claim that they were forgeries and so lost his action. Preventing somebody from 'changing his tune' is an example of the legal principle of estoppel – B was estopped from denying that the cheques were forgeries because of his previous words and actions.

9. To exercise proper care and diligence, especially with regard to the payment and collection of cheques under the Bills of Exchange Act 1882 and the Cheques Act 1957. (We shall return to this subject later.)

10. Where a cheque card has been used correctly with a cheque, then the drawee bank has a duty to pay the cheque and the customer has no right to stop it. However, in general, banks have no obligations to third parties arising out of their duties to pay cheques.

A bank's duty of secrecy

The leading case is *Tournier v National Provincial and Union Bank* (1924). T was employed on a quarterly contract. He was a gambler and had overdrawn his account and failed to keep up the repayments agreed with the bank. The bank phoned him at his office but he was out. The bank then informed T's employer of his gambling and debt to the bank, and the employer, as a result, did not renew T's contract of employment. T sued the bank for breach of contract and won. It was held that the disclosure of T's affairs was a breach of contract because it could not be justified under any of four headings. These four exceptions to the duty of secrecy are:

- When the bank is compelled to disclose the customer's affairs by reason of an Act of Parliament. For instance, the Income Tax Act compels banks to notify the Inland Revenue of customers whose accounts are credited with interest above certain amount, currently about £500 a year. However, the Drug Trafficking Offences Act 1986 contains more important exceptions, for example:

  a) s 24 makes it a criminal offence to hold or control the proceeds of drug trafficking or to assist in the investment of the proceeds, or even to lend money to a drug trafficker. But it is not an offence if a person concerned discloses its knowledge or suspicion and such disclosure is not a breach of its duty of secrecy to its customers.

  b) s 27 provides that the court can issue Production and Access Orders giving the police and Customs access to a bank's records and documents. The customer of the bank must not be advised of the issue of such an order, upon penalty of prosecution for a criminal offence. A bank has seven days in which to comply with an order.

  c) s 28 gives the court the power to issue a search warrant.

  Similar provisions feature in the Prevention of Terrorism (Miscellaneous Provisions) Act 1989, but the penalties on bank officials are more severe.

  More recent legislation requires banks and other financial institutions to report all suspicious transactions to the National Criminal Intelligence Service (NCIS).

- When the bank has a duty of disclosure to the public. In 1924, the example of this duty given in T's case was trading with the enemy. Today, one might have assumed that there was a public duty to reveal drug trafficking but – in view of the fact that one international bank (BCCI) was itself charged, with two subsidiary companies and some staff, with offences relating to drug trafficking by the US Drug Enforcement Agency in 1988 – then it is as well that there is a statutory duty. In any case, the 1986 Act can require such a large amount of staff time in searching the bank's records that, without a statutory duty, it would be very difficult to expect a bank to use its resources in this way.

The Jack Committee regarded this exemption to the duty of secrecy as now being of minimal importance, in view of the many Acts it quoted requiring disclosure of a customer's affairs, nearly all of which had been passed by Parliament since 1924.

- When it is in the bank's interest to disclose the customer's affairs. Thus, when a bank wishes to sue a customer for an unpaid debt it must disclose the balance of the account when requesting the issue of a writ. Another instance might be making enquiries of a customer's relatives or doctor if mental incapacity is suspected. A more dramatic example occurred in May 1988, when the high street banks published advertisements in some national newspapers that they were informing credit reference agencies about persistently defaulting personal customers. Also, some banks now pass names and addresses of customers to their subsidiary companies, who are thus able to sell other financial services by means of direct mail shots to the customers' homes.

- When the customer has given express or implied consent – for instance in giving the bank's name and address as a reference for credit.

  The bankers traditional use of 'implied consent' was tested in *Turner v Royal Bank of Scotland* (1999). RBS had relied on implied consent but T had objected to a reference being sent. The court held that even though the practice was common among banks that was insufficient to bind customers as it 'did not amount to usage'.

Problems may arise with a new practice – the sale for cash of parcels of loans from one bank/mortgage lender to another (securitization).

bank but lost because it had not exercised sufficient care
when drawing and signing the cheque.

- To advise the bank immediately it is discovered that
cheques are being forged. In *Greenwood v Martins Bank*
(1932) the customer delayed notifying the bank for eight
months and was held to be in breach of his duty to inform
the bank immediately the forgeries were discovered.

- When using a cheque card or cash card, which are always
the property of the bank, the customer has a duty to exercise
care, as laid down in the card's conditions of use, which are
on a form signed by the customer. In particular, the cheque
card must be kept away from the cheque book, and the code
number for the cash card (the PIN: personal identification
number) must not be written down anywhere.

- To demand repayment of a credit balance, the customer
must go to the branch of the bank where the account is
maintained, in business hours, and make a demand in
writing. The bank does not have to seek out its creditors.

- Before signing a cheque, the customer must ensure that the
account has sufficient funds or sufficient leeway in the
overdraft limit to meet the cheque.

- To pay reasonable interest and commission and to reimburse
the bank for any costs or losses from operating the account.

In addition, banks have the right to use their customers' deposits as
they see fit, subject to the overall control of the Bank of England.
Also, banks have a lien − a right to retain goods pending the
repayment of an outstanding debt to the bank or the owner of the
goods. This lien includes cheques and securities in the bank's
possession with the exception of goods lodged purely for safe
custody.

Finally, banks can demand immediate repayment of any
overdrawn balance unless notice of repayment can be implied from
the contract that created the debt.

You should also note that, because of the incidence of fraud, firms must also take care to protect themselves from loss if cheques are stolen.

Consider how a thief might amend a cheque payable to 'M&S' to 'M&S Jones' if care is not taken to make Marks & Spencer plc the clear payee.

Additional duties and rights

In the *Turner v RBS* (1999) case we saw that the courts are reluctant to allow banks to add new duties and rights to the banker/customer contract. This follows the ruling in a Hong Kong case by the Privy Council – thus becoming persuasive authority in UK courts. The case was *Tai Hing Cotton Mill Ltd v Liu Chong Hing Bank Ltd* (1986) which involved the forgery of 3,000 cheques. The bank denied liability because the company had not challenged the statements sent to them sharing the forged cheques, contrary to an agreement between the bank and the customer. The Privy Council held that such an agreement placed a burden on the customer which had not been properly highlighted or explained. The bank lost the case.

In this way banks must be very wary of adding new customer duties to the contract and the Banking Code (see later) has been careful not to do this.

The Jack Committee

This report, published in February 1989, recommended among many other matters that a new Banking Service Bill be presented to Parliament to place the rules in Tournier's Case on a statutory footing. The committee was extremely concerned at the erosion of the banks' duty of confidentiality to their customers for direct mail shots, and at the submission to credit reference agencies of information about customers defaulting on unsecured loans of up to £5,000. The report also listed 18 Acts of Parliament breaching the Tournier Rules which had been passed since 1924, and it could find only two Acts that were older than the Tournier case.

Little has been done to implement the report's recommendations, apart from the Cheques Act 1992 and The Deregulation (Bills of Exchange) Order 1996 (which we shall discuss later). However, The Banking Code, the code of practice, can be said to be a result of it.

The Banking Code

From its inception in 1992 The Banking Code has been a voluntary code entered into by banks (there is an equivalent code for Mortgage lenders) as a basis for the 'contract' between a bank and its personal customers. Updated and revised in 1994, 1997 and 2001 the Code has improved customer awareness of bank practice and has given additional protection. An example of this is in the level of loss suffered by customers whose plastic cards have been stolen and misused. Under the Consumer Credit Act 1974 credit cards were protected as loss to the customer was a maximum £50 (provided there was no negligence on the part of the customer). Cards used to access credit balances were not protected at all. The Code put debit cards and credit cards on an equal footing.

The Code also gives customers a proper basis for complaints and is seen to be speedier to react to consumer concerns than the law. In the case *Suriya and Douglas v Midland Bank plc* (1999) the courts did not want to add onerous duties to the bank. In this case advising existing customers that they could obtain better rates of interest on alternative new products. Although the court did not want to add this duty the Code did add it.

The Banking Code covers the following areas:

- 10 key commitments to ensure fairness and openness

- Information about products and services

- Advice of interest rates and changes

- Bank charges (including cash machine charges)

- Running and changing accounts

- Protection such as secrecy and PIN security

- Financial difficulties and complaints

The Code is kept under constant review by The Banking Code Standards Board.

Summary

- A bank is defined in *United Dominions Trust v Kirkwood* and in the Banking Act 1987

- A customer is a person or organization with a current or similar account with a bank.

- Acts of Parliament give banks protection if they act for customers – but not if they act for non-customers – so it is important whether a person is or is not a customer.

- There are five types of legal relationships between banks and customers:

  a) debtor/creditor;

  b) principal/agent;

  c) bailor/bailee;

  d) mortgagor/mortgagee;

  e) special, or fiduciary, where the customer has come to rely on the bank.

- Banks have many duties to their customers:

  a) honouring their cheques up to the credit balance or overdraft limit, provided they are in order and there is no stop;

  b) secrecy – but with the four exceptions outlined in the Tournier Case;

  c) consistency and adherence to the usual course of business;

  d) to give reasonable notice to close an account in credit;

  e) to provide an accurate statement within a reasonable time;

  f) to receive money and cheques for collection and credit customers' accounts with them;

g) to repay credit balances on demand but only after the customer has made demand in writing during business hours at the branch where the account is kept;

h) to advise a customer immediately if it suspects his/her cheques are being forged;

i) to exercise proper care and diligence, especially with cheques;

j) to pay cheques backed by a cheque card;

k) to exercise care when giving advice.

- Customers have duties to their banks:

    a) to take reasonable care when issuing cheques;

    b) to advise the bank immediately they discover their cheques are being forged;

    c) to use cheque cards or cash cards only in accordance with their conditions of use;

    d) to demand repayment of a credit balance only in writing during business hours at the branch where the account is maintained;

    e) to ensure that there are sufficient funds available to meet cheques before they are issued;

    f) to pay reasonable interest and commission;

    g) to allow the bank to use the deposits as it wishes.

- In general, a bank's rights are its customer's duties and vice versa.

- The Banking Code is a voluntary code outlining the banks' basic contract with its customers.

Further Reading – Chapter 7

British Bankers Association (BBA), (2001), *The Banking Code,* BBA.

Arora A, (1993), *Cases and Materials in Banking Law*, Pitman. Chapters 3-5.

Morison IC, (1989), *The Jack Report* (a series of 3 articles), Banking World, May, June and July.

8 Customers and accounts

Objectives

After studying this chapter you should be able to:

- [ ] State the procedures for opening and closing accounts.

- [ ] Give the reasons why these procedures are followed.

- [ ] Identify the various types of personal customers.

- [ ] Explain the advantages and disadvantages of business customers trading as sole traders, partnerships and limited companies.

- [ ] Outline the law concerning limited companies.

- [ ] Outline the procedures for when customers die and companies are wound up.

- [ ] State the Rule in Clayton's case and when it applies.

- [ ] Apply the rules of Combination or Set Off.

Personal customers

Opening accounts

The practice of banks when opening accounts owes much to an understanding of the underlying law as well as the commercial imperative to make the process as speedy as possible for customers. Bank practice has evolved in order to obtain the protection of the Bills of Exchange Act and the Cheques Act 1957 (S4) if the customer pays in cheques which are not his or her property and if the bank is sued for conversion by the rightful owner. Conversion is a tort (a civil law concept and not a crime) occurring when somebody handles another person's property in such a way that the true owner is deprived of his or her right to the property. Thus, conversion can also occur when property is deposited for safe custody with a bank. However, the banks have statutory protection, but this applies only to bills of exchange and cheques and only when the bank acts in good faith and without negligence for a customer.

References from previous bankers or other persons well known to the bank, together with stringent enquiries and application procedures, ought to avoid claims of negligence and, thus, loss of the statutory protection for conversion. Salutary warnings are given by the following cases:

Robinson v Midland Bank Ltd (1925): The account holder must give his or her AUTHORITY for the account to be opened. The banker must either meet the prospective customer or receive the written authority where a third party (eg: a Solicitor) opens the account for them.

Ladbroke v Todd (1914): The bank must be certain of the account holder's IDENTITY. A full passport or driving licence is often sought. Current money laundering regulations also demand at least TWO separate forms of identification.

Marfani v Midland Bank Ltd (1968): The RESPECTABILITY of the customer must be determined. This was made difficult when Marfani wrote his own, glowing, reference. Nowadays references are rare and more proven Credit Scoring methods are used.

Lloyds Bank Ltd v EB Savory & Co (1932): The bank lost its statutory protection because it had failed to obtain details of the husband's occupation and EMPLOYMENT when opening an account for a married woman. Today, in an era of sex equality, it is difficult to apply the rule in Savory's case to all sole accounts of married women. Moreover, the Sex Discrimination Act 1975 makes it illegal for a bank to discriminate against a person by reason of his or her sex.

Importantly, 36 years after the Savory case, in *Marfani & Co Ltd v Midland Bank* (1968) it was stated by the court that the facts known to the banker and the enquiries which he should make must depend on current banking practice and must change with that practice. Hence, cases decided in the first half of the century may not be a reliable guide to the duty of a careful banker at the present time. However, in *Lumsden & Co v London TSB* (1971), the bank did not check on the referee's bankers and was, therefore, held to be negligent. Additionally in *Orbit Mining Ltd v Westminster Bank Ltd* (1963) it was stated that where a customer changes his or her employment the bank has no duty to keep up to date.

However, law and practice began to diverge significantly in about 1965, with many banks at that time requiring only:

a)   identification, such as the production of a current driving licence, and

b)   a search at a credit reference bureau.

During the 1970s and 1980s the banks lost considerable amounts from fraud and bad debts so that measures have been taken to tighten the vetting procedures for people seeking to open current accounts. At the same time competition between retail banks forced many to refuse to respond to references requested by competitors. In many banks, application forms for current accounts are not available from the literature dispensers in their branches, while TV advertisements do not feature current accounts so prominently. Many of the new type of current accounts now being offered include small automatic overdraft facilities and so are regulated agreements under the Consumer Credit Act 1974. These require considerable documentation, which incorporate details from which Credit Scoring can be performed.

In April 1994, new regulations came into effect, as part of the campaign against 'laundering' the cash proceeds of crime into bank and building society accounts. In effect, this cleans or launders the illegal proceeds, so that trace of its origins cannot be found: the origin was a deposit of cash. The recent changes extend to the proceeds of all criminal activities and make it a criminal offence for a bank or building society not to have rules to combat money laundering. The Drug Trafficking Act 1994 consolidates all the relevant legislation.

Accordingly, all banks and building societies now insist upon, when an account is opened even if it is to remain in credit, the following procedure:

- completion of the application form;

Figure 6
Modern account opening procedures

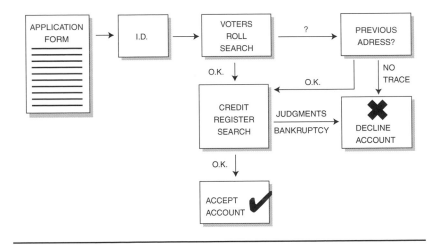

- a valid passport or driving licence, which verifies the person's signature;

- a very recent bill or statement from, say, another bank, British Gas or an H.P. company, confirming the person's address;

- a search on the voters' roll and a clear credit reference search.

Cash and cheques issued by other people will not be accepted until the address has been checked with the Electoral Register. As Electoral Registers are not always up to date a previous address may also be sought.

Closing accounts

If the account is in credit, the bank must give reasonable notice to the customer: (see *Prosperity Ltd v Lloyds Bank* (1923) earlier) for personal accounts the notice given is usually one month. Where an account has been improperly conducted, eg where cheques for large amounts have been drawn against uncleared effects, it may be closed at shorter notice.

Accounts in default or overdrawn are 'on demand' and can be closed without notice. In practice, however, banks allow customers a reasonable time to make alternative banking arrangements.

The use of cheque guarantee cards and debit cards (see Chapter 9) also cautions delay. Debits generated by these mechanisms are normally guaranteed by the issuing bank and so the bank must be sure that there are no items outstanding upon closure that would subsequently have to be paid.

Events occurring during the customer's life

Mental incapacity

This terminates the bank's mandate to operate the customer's account. His or her relatives should apply to the Court of Protection for the appointment of a receiver to handle the customer's affairs, as provided in the Mental Health Act 1983. The exception is where an enduring power of attorney was executed when the customer was of sound mind (see later in this chapter).

The receiver may open an account and, if he or she is unknown, then references should be taken. The appointment of the receiver should be recorded in the probate register used to maintain a record of events in the lives of customers and the original appointment document should be seen. An ordinary photocopy is not acceptable because forgery is so easy.

Death

This also terminates the bank's mandate to operate the account and cheques must be returned marked 'drawer deceased' after the bank has received notice of the customer's death. The bank will need to see the original death certificate or an official copy, and will be reluctant to act merely on a telephone call from a relative who may be unknown to the bank. In the past, death notices in respected newspapers have been used as evidence of a customer's demise.

If the customer had only a sole account, any credits received after notice of the death should be placed to the credit of a new account in the name of 'Personal representatives of X deceased'. Joint accounts, which are discussed shortly, continue in the name of the surviving parties.

Bankruptcy

This is regulated by the Insolvency Act 1986, which provides various ways to give statutory protection to people or companies whose debts (liabilities to creditors) greatly exceed their assets. The assets of the debtor are gathered in by an independent person known as the trustee in bankruptcy or liquidator. Sometimes this is a civil servant, known as the Official Receiver, but more frequently he (or she) is an accountant specializing in such matters and known as a licensed insolvency practitioner. There are many stages of insolvency but, as soon as a court makes a bankruptcy order, the Official Receiver becomes the debtor's trustee or liquidator in bankruptcy, unless a licensed practitioner is later appointed.

Immediately after the bankruptcy order is made, the Official Receiver contacts the branch, informing the manager that a bankruptcy order has been made against a customer. The account must be frozen, whether it is in debit or credit, and all cheques presented after notice of the order was received must be returned, marked 'Refer to drawer, bankruptcy order made'. Details of the order will be published in London Gazette, a government publication, which is read by banks and credit reference bureaux to discover which of their customers, etc, are now bankrupt – and so it is not libellous to write this information on a cheque.

If the bank is owed money by the bankrupt it will need to exercise its remedies under any security it may hold or submit proof of the debt to the Trustee in due course to obtain repayment. For unsecured debt the likelihood of full repayment is very remote. More detail in insolvency and banks is given in Chapter 14.

Marriage or Change of Name

If a customer changes his or her name on marriage then the bank should ask to see the marriage certificate, for recording in the probate register. The separate taxation of married women, which began in April 1990, has led to special consideration being given to ensure that they pay as little income tax as possible (see later). The Cheques Act 1992, which obliges banks to collect cheques marked Account Payee for the named payee only, also makes this event and a change of name by Deed Poll important. No longer can wedding guests present cheques to 'Mr & Mrs Newlywed' or 'The Bride and Groom' without causing problems.

Agency

A customer can appoint an agent in several ways to operate his or her bank account:

1. A per procuriam authority to operate the account can be completed on one of the bank's standard forms. This may stipulate whether the agent can overdraw the account and, if so, to what limit. Death, mental incapacity or bankruptcy of the customer will terminate the agent's authority to sign on the account. However, if the agent dies, then any cheques he or she had signed may be paid, provided that they are in order.

2.   Signing a power of attorney, which is a wide-ranging authority for a third party to manage the whole of a person's affairs. The regulating statute is the Powers of Attorney Act 1971. The deed of appointment must be seen by the bank and recorded in the probate register. The death, mental incapacity or bankruptcy of the donor – the person appointing the attorney – terminate the deed.

The Enduring Powers of Attorney Act 1985 created a new type of power of attorney, given before and in anticipation of the donor's eventual mental incapacity. At the time of appointment, the donor must be in full possession of his or her mental faculties; the attorney may use the power but, when the donor becomes incapable or the attorney suspects that the donor is incapable, then the power must be registered with the Court of Protection. The attorney may not act again until the power is registered and both the original deed of appointment and its registration must be recorded in the branch probate register.

Joint accounts

These are accounts in the names of two or more people (known as the parties), excluding the accounts of trustees, partnerships and personal representatives of dead people – all of which we shall mention later. The bank's mandate for joint accounts will specify:

- who will sign cheques – whether all, some or any party;

- joint and several liability of all parties for debit balances on the account;

- that if one party dies then the remainder can authorize the release of funds.

Thus, if a husband dies – and many husbands die before their wives die – then his widow can continue to operate the former joint account, which then becomes automatically a sole account in her name.

The parties to a joint account are, under the general law, jointly liable for any borrowing. Following the Civil Liability (Contribution) Act 1978, joint liability has meant that the bank can sue all parties, individually and collectively, for repayment of any borrowing, so that if there are X parties then there are X + 1 rights of action. The extra right of action is to sue all the parties collectively.

Joint and several liability, upon which a bank insists, gives a bank the right to combine any credit balances on sole accounts in the name of any of the parties to the joint account with the debit balance on that joint account. Joint and several liability also means that the estates of any of the parties who have died are liable for the debt on the joint account.

If one of the parties becomes bankrupt, then the joint account must be frozen. The solvent party or parties must be contacted and new accounts (sole if necessary), excluding the bankrupt person, must be opened. The authority of any solvent parties should be sought to debit the new account with the cheques which they had drawn on the now frozen joint account.

Married women

Since the Sex Discrimination Act 1975 it is illegal to discriminate against anybody on the grounds of his or her sex. Hence, it is difficult to establish the name of the employer of the husbands of married women seeking to open bank accounts in credit, so most banks have dispensed with this requirement, although it is possible to re-introduce it by using the word 'partners' which applies to husband, wife or person with whom the applicant is living. However, when lending is involved, it is now customary for both men and women to give details of their partner's employment and income – as required by stores and credit companies when granting credit.

Divorce

Where a bank receives notice of extreme tension between marriage or joint account partners, it may be necessary for the bank to insist that cheques drawn on a joint account are signed by both husband

and wife, irrespective of the mandate. Often the family house has to be sold in order to provide a fair distribution of their assets.

This action is prudent in two practical ways: It avoids the bank becoming a 'referee' between warring couples and it can avoid the worst effects of the financial pressure on individuals brought about by divorce.

Minors

Minors are people under the age of 18, following the Family Law Reform Act 1969. Before this Act the age was 21. Minors are not liable on many contracts made before they are 18 and so there may be legal complications if they have bank accounts, because the main legal relationship between a bank and its customer is a contractual one as debtor and creditor.

The acceptability to a bank of a minor to operate a current account will depend on:

a)   the minor's circumstances, and

b)   the bank's marketing policy. Present-day practice is to offer a current account and cheque book when the minor reaches 16. Cheque cards will be issued at that age only when the banking connection justifies it.

Children under 16 are usually offered some form of savings account. When they are under 7, their parents will operate the account but after that age they will be able to withdraw from the account against their own signature. ATM cards are now available on such accounts when the youngster is 13 or over, but the written permission of a parent is usually required before a card is issued.

Under the Minors' Contracts Act 1987 minors can assume liability for contracts made before they were 18, once they are over 18. Otherwise they are only liable to pay for necessaries, eg food. Their bank borrowing can now be guaranteed and the guarantor sued. Previously the bank had to insist on an indemnity being given.

Under the Consumer Credit Act 1974 it is an offence to grant credit within the terms of the Act to a minor, so a credit card cannot be issued. Neither can a debit card if it involves some form of credit or overdraft.

For income tax purposes, most minors (unless they are very rich) should avoid having large balances in accounts where income tax is deducted at source from the interest.

Business and other accounts

Sole traders

These are individuals trading in their own name, although they may have a number of employees. The main disadvantage of being a sole trader is that he or she is personally liable for all business debts without limit, so that the family house may have to be sold to pay the creditors. Sometimes, a sole trader will place the house into the name of the spouse to try to avoid such a situation occurring.

A second disadvantage is that sole traders frequently have difficulty in obtaining credit, especially trade credit from their suppliers. Unlike companies, they do not have to publish accounts or file any documents with the government so that it is hard to find out anything about their business affairs.

A third disadvantage is that, if a sole trader is ill and has no reliable employee who can run the business, then sales will dry up and the trader may be forced out of business.

The major advantage is independence, especially when compared to being an employee. Also, the income tax due on trading profits is assessed by the Inland Revenue on a very different basis from the way wages and salaries are assessed. The latter are taxed under what is called Schedule E, against which very few expenses can be claimed. However trading profits are assessed under what is called Schedule D, against which such items as travelling expenses and clerical help can be claimed.

A second advantage is the lack of formality. No document has to be drawn up or annual returns made and meetings do not have to be held each year. However, the laws concerning health and safety at work, etc, still have to be observed.

Many sole traders have a separate bank account for their business – perhaps called 'Shop Account'. The legal formalities for these accounts are virtually the same as for personal sole accounts.

There is one practical difference – charges are levied on a separate business tariff published by the bank.

Partnerships

Partnership is the legal relationship between people carrying on a business in common with a view to profit. Most partnerships are limited to a maximum of 20 partners but there can be a higher limit, and partnerships of solicitors, accountants and members of the Stock Exchange may be of unlimited size.

The bank account is conducted in the name of the partnership, eg 'Lipscombe, Pond & Co' and the mandate – the form instructing the bank who is to sign cheques – must be signed by every partner. The mandate will incorporate joint and several liability of all the partners for any debts to the bank because their liability under the Partnership Act 1890 is only joint.

A deed of partnership is usually drawn up. However, there is no necessity for there to be a deed establishing a partnership because the relationship can be inferred from the behaviour of the partners. Some banks do not ask to see the deed if the account is to be in credit but if borrowing is anticipated it is then advisable to see the deed, photocopy it and enter it in the probate register.

On the death of a partner, an overdrawn bank account is frozen and a new account opened for the surviving partners. The admission of a new partner to the partnership should be confirmed in writing by all the other partners and the new partner should also confirm that he or she accepts joint or several liability for any overdrawn account.

Sometimes limited partnerships are formed, where either or some, but not all, of the partners limit their liability for the debts of the firm.

Companies

Companies have a legal identity separate from their shareholders (their owners) and nearly all have limited liability for their shareholders. This is the meaning of 'limited company' because the shareholders are not liable for any of the debts of the company if it should fail. It is a great advantage, although there is some form-filling and cost involved in setting up a company.

This fundamental principle of company law was established in *Salomon v Salomon & Co Ltd* (1897). S Ltd had issued a special type of security called 'secured debentures' to Mr Salomon, who was the major shareholder in S Ltd. These debentures enabled Mr. S to 'go to the head of the queue of creditors' when the company failed. Therefore the other creditors received little. Naturally, they were dissatisfied, claiming that S and S Ltd were really one and the same person. They sued for more money and, at first, won. However, they did not succeed in the House of Lords which held that S Ltd was a separate legal person from its shareholders so that Mr S could be a secured creditor and thereby get his money back before the other creditors got theirs.

Company documents

Companies have three documents of concern to bankers:

1. A certificate of incorporation which is issued by the Registrar of Companies and certifies that the company meets the requirements of the Companies Act. At present, the relevant Act is the Companies Act 1985. Older companies are governed by earlier Companies Acts, such as those of 1929 and 1948.

2. A memorandum of association which determines the company's relations with the rest of the world, ie its name, the location of its registered office (not the same as the Head Office, which can be moved without changing the memorandum of association) and its objects clause. The latter is usually drafted as widely as possible because the company cannot enter into any contracts which are not permitted under its objects clause. The Companies Act 1989 abolished the *ultra vires* rule (beyond the company's powers) as the UK moves into line with the rest of the EU, where the rule does not apply to companies. In this way banks no longer need to be concerned that a company is acting outside its powers. In the past this has invalidated loans, leaving banks with losses when revealed that the company had no legal power to borrow for the specific purpose.

3.   Articles of association which regulate a company's internal operations such as the borrowing powers of the directors, voting procedures, etc. Each major Companies Act contains a specimen set of articles of association, known as Table A, which a company can adopt if it wishes.

Plcs (see below) also need a fourth document – a trading certificate or certificate to commence business, as it is sometimes known, issued by the Registrar of Companies.

Public and private companies
Companies are divided into two main categories – public for the larger companies and private for the smaller. The distinctions were changed in 1980, to harmonize with procedures in the rest of the European Union.
    Public limited companies (Plcs) must have:

- Shares which are capable of being transferred without restriction;

- A share capital for an authorized amount of £50,000 or more, of which at least £50,000 must have been issued (issued capital can be less than authorized);

- At least two shareholders.

All other companies are private limited companies ('Limited' or 'Ltd'). Many of these were incorporated before 1985 and hence have articles that comply with earlier legislation, eg a maximum of 50 shareholders, or restrictions on the right of shareholders to transfer their shares without the directors' approval.
    There is another type of company – one limited by guarantee, whereby the members undertake to pay a nominal sum, eg £1 each, to guarantee the company's debts. Since the Companies Act 1985 no company limited by guarantee can have a share capital and it must, therefore, be a private company. Such companies are used by sports clubs to run a bar or by charities to run their trading activities.

Opening a company's bank account

There should be no need for references, because company accounts are usually introduced by directors, solicitors or accountants already known to the bank.

The following must be obtained by the bank and recorded in the appropriate file:

- The certificate of incorporation;

- The memorandum and articles of association. Copies should be held in the authorities' file at the branch and it is good practice to write once in every five years for an up-to-date copy of the articles in case they have been amended without the bank being aware;

- The trading certificate, if the company is a Plc. Before this is produced by the company, the bank should allow only credits to the company's account;

- A copy of the board resolution passed by the directors appointing the bank as the company's bankers;

- The bank's mandate detailing who is to sign cheques and endorse bills, etc.

Solicitors

The Law Society is the governing body for solicitors and requires them to pay all money belonging to their clients into separate bank accounts designated Clients' Accounts, which must never be overdrawn.

Under the Solicitors' Accounts Rules and the Law Society's Guide to Professional Conduct (1999), the solicitor must pay the client's money into a deposit account if the amount held exceeds: £1000 for eight weeks; £2,000 for four weeks; £10,000 for two weeks, or £20,000 for one week. Interest on clients' funds must also be accounted for where this exceeds £20.

If the solicitor is acting as a trustee then there must be a bank account entitled either 'executor' or 'trustee' into which the money is paid.

For day-to-day office administration there will be an 'office account', on which an overdraft limit may be granted if appropriate.

Other professionals

Other professionals who regularly hold clients funds, such as Insurance Brokers; Insurance Companies; Financial Advisors and Intermediaries and Estate Agents are governed by numerous codes of conduct and statutory rules regarding separation of clients funds.

Insurance Brokers are governed by the Insurance Brokers' Registration Council, Insurance Companies by the voluntary General Insurance Standards Council, Financial firms by the Financial Services Authority and Estate Agents by the Office of Fair Trading.

Clubs and associations

These have no separate legal identity and their business affairs are conducted by the members in a general meeting or are delegated to an executive committee.

A separate bank account for the club/association is strongly advisable in order to avoid a treasurer or secretary mixing his or her own money with that of the club or association; if the account is termed 'J Bloggs A/c Orchard Road School PTA' then Mr Bloggs will be personally liable for any overdraft and the bank is given notice of a trust.

The bank's standard mandate for such clubs and association should be used, appointing the bank as bankers and authorising the chairman, secretary and treasurer 'for the time being' to sign cheques.

Lending is possible to a club, against third-party security, eg charges by members over their own property. The death of a signatory does not affect the operation of the account, although for practical reasons he or she should be replaced.

Some large clubs, eg sports clubs, may be companies limited by guarantee.

Executors and administrators

An executor is appointed by the will of a person who has died, and carries out the instructions contained in the will. An administrator is appointed by the court, usually there is no will but this also occurs where the person named as executor cannot or does not wish to act.

The executor obtains a document called a grant of probate from the court to distribute the dead person's assets (his or her estate), according to the will. The administrator obtains letters of administration to deal with the estate according to the law of intestacy (where there is no will and which give a large share to the widow or widower and much of the remainder to the children). If there is a will but no executor, then the administrator obtains a grant of letters of administration with the will annexed.

However, before probate is granted and this distribution can begin, inheritance tax (IHT) must be paid if the net estate is (at present) £242,000 or more. Often, this payment is financed by a bank loan, repaid from the sale of part or all of the estate. The Inland Revenue will accept the payment by instalments of that part of IHT arising from real property. Also, the executor can pay IHT direct from the deceased's National Savings.

After a year – called the executor's year – the estate should have been wound up, with all creditors paid and the net assets distributed according to the will or the laws of intestacy. If there is a trust involved in the will, then the executor/s become trustees so the bank should make enquiries after the end of the year if the account is still being operated. If a trust exists, then a new mandate should be obtained, with all executors/trustees signing.

Executors can delegate their powers (unlike trustees) and so not all of them need sign cheques.

Trustees

Trustees deal with property that is under their control for the benefit of others – the beneficiaries. Trustees are appointed by a trust deed.

If there is an account in the name of 'J Brown, re Jane Green' or 'Joe Bloggs, Treasurer of Orchard Road School PTA' then the bank may have indirect notice of a trust. If a bank has notice of a trust – either directly when the trustees open an account as trustees or indirectly, as mentioned above – it can run the danger of being party to a breach of trust. The beneficiary(i.e.s) can then sue the bank for damages.

When trustees open a bank account, the bank ought to see the trust deed and cheques should be signed by all trustees. As we mentioned in the previous section, trustees cannot delegate their powers.

If borrowing is needed, eg to run a business for the benefit of the beneficiary, then specific authority for this must be given in the will or trust deed.

When one trustee dies, the remainder continue to act. Strangely, bankruptcy does not remove a trustee, unless a co-trustee applies to the court for the removal of the bankrupt trustee.

There are now more than 130,000 charities and many of them are trusts, while others are companies limited by guarantee. A will is also a form of trust.

Managing bank accounts

Clayton's case

You should have noticed references to 'freezing the account' when certain events occur to an overdrawn account and you should have asked yourselves: 'Why do we have to do this?'

The answer is that an old but very important case laid down a principle – known as the Rule in Clayton's case (*Devaynes v Noble* (1816)) – which requires us to do so, if we wish to keep the bank's rights. These rights are to sue one or more of the following:

- a guarantor;

- a partner;

- a joint account holder;

- a third party who has charged their own security to secure the customer's borrowing;

- the estates of any of the above, after their deaths or the death of the customer.

The Rule in Clayton's case states that credits are appropriated or 'matched against' the debit items usually in the same order in which the debit items were dated. Let us take an example from the bank account of a partnership – P Igeon and B Luetit.

Following the Rule, the three payments into the account of £100 have extinguished the two debits made on 13 and 27 January. Mr Luetit died on 31 January, and the debt of £300 then outstanding would be repaid by the three subsequent credits. His estate would not have been liable for this £300 after 1 March, when the third credit was made. Thereafter, the bank would have to look to Mr Igeon for the repayment of any debt.

Figure 8
Clayton's case in action

University Bank plc

——————— 1 The Campus, Oxbridge ———————

Statement of Account
Account of P Igeon and B Luetit
Account No. 12345678

Date 2000	Item	Debit	Credit	Balance £ Credit C Debit D
Jan 13	Cheque	100		100 D
Jan 27	Cheque	200		300 D
Mr Luetit died on 31 January				
Feb 3	Cheque	300		600 D
Feb 10	Credit		100	500 D
Feb 17	Credit		100	400 D
Feb 24	Cheque	200		600 D
Mar 1	Credit		100	500 D

However, if the account had been frozen at Dr £300 on 31 January, and a new account opened that day, then by 1 March the bank would have been owed £300 by Mr Igeon and the estate of Mr Luetit, together with £200 owed by Mr Igeon alone. It might well be that Mr Igeon could not repay the £500 he owes in total, being able to repay only the £200, leaving £300 for the bank to claim from Mr Luetit's estate.

So, by freezing or ruling off the current account, the bank should be in a better position than it would have been by letting the account continue. It certainly is not in a worse position.

Events which cause the Rule to jeopardise a bank's position include:

- Death or insolvency of a partner, joint account holder, guarantor, or person who has charged third-party security.

- Death or insolvency of a customer whose borrowing is guaranteed or is secured by property charged by a third party.

The Rule can be overridden if either the borrower or the lender stipulates the exact debit items against which the credits are to be appropriated or 'matched'. (You will learn more about this later in your studies.)

Fortunately, there are many cases where the Rule does not apply. Thus, with a loan account there is usually only one debit, so all credits go towards extinguishing that item, or towards repayment of interest charges. Moreover, it does not affect the bank adversely when the borrowing is on a sole account and security has been charged by the customer.

Appropriation
A further application of The Rule in Clayton's case was seen in *Deeley v Lloyds Bank Ltd* (1912) where it was stated that the person paying funds into an account (debtor) has the primary right to say to what account it shall be appropriated; the creditor (bank) if the debtor makes no appropriation, has the right to appropriate; and if neither of them exercises the right The Rule in Clayton's case applies.

Bankers are often faced with the problem of deciding which cheques to pay and which to return unpaid where there are insufficient funds in the account to pay them all. The Deeley case shows that the bank has the right to choose where the debtor is silent. This is subject to the bank's overriding duty of care to the customer also.

Cheque Truncation (see later) foresees that only basic dates on a cheque (cheque number, sort code, account number and amount) will be transmitted to a paying bank. Banks are, therefore, collaborating on an image archive for cheques in order to be able to satisfy their duty of care by distinguishing between cheques using payees' names.

Combination or set off

The bankers right of combination or set off arises when the net indebtedness of the customer is calculated. Whether on a running account or at the termination of the banker customer relationship the bank has the right to combine balances on accounts at the same branch or at different branches of the same bank. This follows *Foley v Hill* which established that the banker customer contract is basically that of debtor/creditor.

For set off to apply three basic rules must be observed:

The amounts to set off must be CERTAIN, they must be in accounts of the SAME NAME and the accounts must be held in the SAME RIGHT OR CAPACITY.

An example of this can arise on the death of a customer where the following accounts and balances are held:

I.M.Deceased current a/c	£2,500 Dr	FROZEN
I.M.Deceased loan a/c	£5,000 Dr	UNSECURED
I.M Deceased & R Survivor (joint current account)	£4,000 Cr	TRANSFERRED TO SURVIVOR
I.M.Deceased deposit account	£1,000 Cr	FROZEN
I.M.Deceased, Trustee for A Child deposit account	£1,500 Cr	FROZEN

The net indebtedness to the bank is £6,500 because only the sole deposit account can be set off against the debit balances. The joint account survivor is not responsible for sole debts of the deceased (only for those on the joint account) and the trust account cannot be touched because it is not held in the SAME CAPACITY as the other accounts. The bank will need to look to the Executors or Administrators of the estate to repay the balance of the debt.

If, however, the joint account had been overdrawn the credit money standing on the account of I.M.Deceased could have been used to pay off the debt.

Summary

- Due care must be taken when an account is opened if the protection given to the bank by Acts of Parliament is to be available.

- Care must be taken to check the customer's identity and address: two forms of identification are now used.

- Special procedures must be followed when a customer becomes mentally incapable of handling his or her affairs, or dies, or becomes bankrupt or appoints an agent or attorney.

- The accounts of married women and people under the age of 18 require special consideration.

- Banks usually ensure that parties to joint bank accounts are severally as well as jointly liable for debit balances. Since 1978 the $(X + 1)$ rights of action for joint and several liability are also available for joint liability but there are still two advantages for joint and several liability – the parties' estates are liable and credit balances in their sole names can be set-off against a debt on a joint account. Similarly, banks insist on joint and several liability for partnership accounts.

- Companies have to produce three documents when a bank account is opened for them – certificate of incorporation, memorandum of association and articles of association. Plcs also have to produce a fourth: their certificate to commence business.

- There are now four types of people looking after insolvent companies – liquidators, receivers, administrators and supervisors. For individuals there are trustees in bankruptcy and supervisors.

- Executors of wills are appointed by the will of the dead person; administrators of estates are appointed by the court. Both can delegate (authorize others to act for them).

- Trustees have an overriding duty to look after property for the benefit of somebody else – and cannot delegate.

- The Rule in Clayton's case explains why accounts are frozen.

- Mutual dealings and accounts in debit and credit can give rise to a right of combination or set off.

Further Reading – Chapter 8

Arora A, (1997), *Practical Banking and Building Society Law,* Blackstone Press. Chapters 6, 7 and 9.

Wadsley J, and Penn G (2000), *The Law Relating to Domestic Banking,* (2nd edition), Sweet & Maxwell. Chapters 3, 8 and 9.

9   Payment methods

Objectives

After studying this chapter you should be able to:

☐   Describe the various methods of payment used by personal customers in the UK.

☐   State which is the preferred method of payment for various transactions.

☐   Describe some of the methods of payment used by tourists and business people when travelling abroad.

Introduction

The payments market has seen numerous changes over recent years as banks (and retailers) try to convert to plastic card transactions while many customers still prefer cash. Business users have shown a preference for cheques in the past and this is reflected in the large amount of paper still in use in the payments systems. Business users are slowly starting to use automated payment methods. These trends are set to continue over the next five years, at least, and new developments are on the horizon (see later) to change the way we pay for goods and services.

The various methods of payment in common use are described below.

Cash

There are many ways of paying debts, and here we mean debts within the UK, owed by personal customers. Some of these ways – cash and cheques – are also used by big organizations, which can also use electronic methods.

Figure 8
Payment preferences in 2000 (APACS)

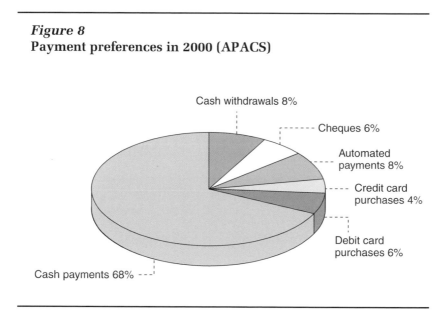

Cash withdrawals 8%

Cheques 6%

Automated payments 8%

Credit card purchases 4%

Debit card purchases 6%

Cash payments 68%

Cash is the oldest method of payment and is still used in the majority of transactions, most of which are for small amounts. The Coinage Acts specify what must be accepted when tendered or offered in payments of certain sums. Here is a reminder of the values:

- Bronze coins (1p and 2p) are legal tender for up to 20p.

- Cupro nickel coins (5p 10p 20p) are legal tender for up to £5.

- 50p coins are legal tender for up to £10.

- £1 and £2 coins are legal tender for any amount.

Bank of England notes are, of course, legal tender for any amount. In February 2000 £25 billion of notes were in circulation with around £1.3 billion being renewed each year. In theory, we must tender the exact amount. Change is given by the creditor, the person to whom we owe the money, only as a matter of courtesy.

Cash, however, is bulky and can be stolen. Thus, it is slowly losing its popularity and being replaced by other methods of payments. But cash has one great advantage – it 'leaves no traces' and can quite often be passed from hand to hand without entries in books of account. For instance, in a supermarket the till records all payments in and out, including change given, but in a street market the cash usually goes straight into the trader's money-apron. For this reason, cash is preferred when buyers and sellers seek to avoid paying income tax and VAT. Although handling of large amounts of cash is not illegal it can raise suspicions, especially where this is not a normal account activity. Drug traffickers are known to use cash for transactions (see Chapter 7).

Lastly, the Bank of England works hard to make forgery of banknotes and coins difficult, yet this does still occur. Under the forgery and Counterfeiting Act 1981 it is illegal to hold a forged banknote – this must be reported to and given up to the police immediately. This causes a loss for the person holding it – hence the sign seen in shops 'we do not accept £50 notes' and the use of ultra-violet lights to authenticate genuine notes.

Cheques

A cheque is defined as an instruction in writing to a banker ordering him to pay a third party the amount stated. (See next chapter for a detailed look at this definition.)

Cheques have been a popular method of payment, particularly if used in conjunction with a cheque guarantee card. For very small amounts they are not acceptable and, many shops will not accept them for £5 or less. The reason for this unwillingness to accept cheques for small-value transactions is that the traders may have to pay bank charges of between 8p and 65p for each cheque paid into their bank. This compares with 50p per £100 for cash handling.

For anybody who accepts a cheque there can be problems. First, has the person enough funds in the account or will the cheque be returned unpaid for lack of funds? Second, is the person offering it the true owner of the cheque or will it be returned unpaid, marked 'signature differs' or 'orders not to pay' or 'no account'? Third, is the cheque correctly drawn or will it be returned marker 'out of date' or 'words and figures differ'?

In spite of these problems, cheques are widely used because they are easier for traders to transport than cash and are certainly less attractive to thieves. The latter prefer cash every time!

Without the backing of cheque cards, cheques are still widely accepted for certain types of transactions. For example, where the goods are to be delivered after payment has been made and the cheque cleared; where the customer and his or her address are known to the shopkeeper/trader, eg a newsagent who delivers papers daily or a mail-order transaction with a catalogue holder; where the customer and the supplier have a long-standing relationship; where the item being paid for relates to the customer's house, eg quarterly gas and electricity bills.

Cheques are preferred by business users for reasons of convenience and because cheques allow businesses to enjoy a 'float' while a cheque is being cleared and before it is applied to a bank account. A cheque also provides evidence of receipt and evidence of non-payment should it be returned unpaid.

Cheque guarantee cards

In the mid-1960s the banks developed the system of cheque guarantee cards which, when used with a cheque, guarantees that the cheque will not be returned for lack of funds, thereby avoiding the problems mentioned above. At first, the limit of the guarantee was £30 but so great has been the amount of fraud involving guarantee cards that the banks felt only able to increase the limit only once – in 1977 – to £50. In April 1989, however, the banks agreed to have a variable limit for cheque cards, which can now be issued with a guarantee of £100 or even £250, at a bank's discretion. Moreover, building societies now issue their own cheque guarantee cards, some of which have a £250 guarantee. In effect there is now a range of limits, from £50 to £250.

The common feature of all cheque guarantee cards is the hologram of William Shakespeare, and they can now incorporate debit and credit card features (see later).

Procedure at the point of sale

- The customer signs the cheque in front of the shop assistant, who checks that the signature on the cheque is the same as that on the guarantee card. The amount of the cheque must not exceed the cheque card guarantee limit and the cheque must be the only cheque issued for the transaction.

- The shop assistant must then check that the card bears the same name and signature as the cheque, that the card has not been altered or defaced and that it has not passed its expiry date.

- The assistant then writes the number of the cheque card on the back of the cheque.

- The card is then handed back to the customer, with the goods and receipt.

The customer has no right to stop a cheque used with a cheque guarantee card since this would breach both the contract between the bank and its customer and the contract of guarantee between the bank and the payee. The guaranteed cheque will also be paid even where the drawer is dead!

Where traders wish to accept cheques above the cheque-card limit the cheque is not guaranteed by the bank. Since many cheques exceed the limit Transax Financial Services Ltd have exploited the area. Transax considers guaranteeing any cheque accepted by its members (membership around £30 per month). Transax uses a unique database of 8.5 million transaction records and boasts that over 98% of all requests are guaranteed. The guarantee is issued in seconds as the trader phones Transax with the details. If the cheque is unpaid (bounced) the trader does not lose out.

Cheque card fraud and misuse

In 2000 UK plastic card fraud totalled £293m, an alarming rise from the level of £188m in 1999. This is a worrying problem for retailers, banks and the police but the reduction in cheque usage by personal customers and the better security in use by card issuers should further reduce this figure in the future. Cheque Card fraud accounted for a £9m loss in 2000.

Unlike a cheque book, a cheque card remains the property of the bank, so that a thief could be prosecuted under the Theft Act 1968 for stealing a card.

In *R v Kovacs* (1974) (R = Regina = the Queen, a term used for the prosecution in criminal cases) the customer stated that there were no cheques left after being requested to return her cheque book and cheque card because her account was overdrawn. Two months later, she issued two more cheques, which further overdrew her account. On prosecution she was found guilty of obtaining by deception under the Theft Act 1968. A conviction for deception was also found in *Metropolitan Police Commissioner v Charles* (1976), which related to the original £30 limit on a cheque card at the time when the banks' conditions for the use of cheque cards did not contain a restriction of one cheque for £30 (now £50 or more) for any one transaction. Using his cheque card, the customer cashed all 25 cheques in his book on one evening's gambling, incurring an unauthorized overdraft as a result of the bank's obligation to honour all the cheques.

A shock was delivered to banks, however, in *First Sport Ltd v Barclays* (1992). Although First Sport had accepted a stolen cheque card and cheque as payment for goods, since the signature of the fraudster was a good replica of the true customer Barclays had to honour the cheque. Barclays' card agreement with retailers was worded in a way to protect retailers acting in good faith in these circumstances. Banks accordingly made changes to their card agreements to avoid a similar claim in the future.

To reduce losses arising from fraud and misuse of cheque cards, the banks take a number of precautions. These include:

- Not issuing cards to new or inexperienced customers, until they seem to be trustworthy.

- Not allowing customers to use the card to overdraw accounts without prior arrangement (eg by refusing to issue a new cheque book).

- Offering training and advice to retailers and their staff.

- Requiring customers to keep their cards separate from their cheque books. (This is easier for those who have several pockets in their coats and trousers but not for those who usually keep everything in their handbags or briefcases.) Some banks put Mr/Mrs/Miss/Ms on their cheque books and cheque cards to prevent them being used by a thief of the opposite sex.

- Inserting a clause in the 'conditions of use of cards' that ownership of the card remains with the bank.

- Reducing the number of cheques in a cheque book. This is now usually 25, rather than 30 or more.

- For cheque cards with a £100 guarantee, a bank or building society may take extra precautions, such as requiring the customer to collect the card from the branch, rather than sending it by post to the customer.

- Some banks have pioneered laser-etched customer photos on cards.

- Banks distribute 'Hot card' files to retailers electronically. These list known stolen cards.

- Perhaps the best protection in the future will be the incorporation of a micro-chip into a card to allow identification.

Debit cards

These were introduced in 1987. As a method of payment they act both as a cheque guarantee card for cheques and as a 'reusable cheque' for any amount. Increasingly retailers are electronically linked to banks in order to obtain on-line authorization for higher-level payments (typically over £50), to access details of the latest stolen cards and to send transactions electronically for accounts to be updated. Thus, the length of time taken for the debit to reach the customer's account can be instantaneous. The cards are subject to the Consumer Credit Act 1974 if an overdraft facility is included in the product package and therefore cannot be issued to people under 18. They also have a third use – as an ATM card (see below).

Debit card fraud totalled £86.1m in 2000, a 57% rise on 1999. An estimated 36% of all plastic card fraud takes place using counterfeit cards and a further 34% with lost or stolen cards.

Midland, National Westminster and Royal Bank of Scotland have an electronic debit card, SWITCH, which uses no paper to reach the bank account. SWITCH was the first debit card to be accepted at Sainsbury's, where it uses the electronic terminals at the check-outs. Paper is still involved, however, because the customer signs a voucher which authenticates the transaction and acts as a receipt. The SWITCH banks also issue SOLO cards although no overdraft is allowed on these.

All debit cards issued in the 1980s were linked to VISA because of its more flexible membership policy and because it permitted member banks to approach retailers directly to request them to accept the cards, rather than use an independent sales force, as with the now defunct Access.

Finally, note that debit cards are neither credit cards nor charge cards, because all transactions are debited to the appropriate bank account.

ATM cards

ATM stands for automated teller machine, 'teller' being the American and Scottish word for cashier. Such cards are issued to customers, on completion of an application form, and a confidential four-digit personal identification number (PIN) is sent separately a few days after the card. When the customer acknowledges, in writing, receipt of the PIN, the computer is instructed to permit cash withdrawals. These are activated by the card and authenticated by the PIN number being keyed in at the ATM.

The first generation of ATM cards were plastic cards to permit withdrawals from cash dispensers away from branch counters. They now also enable statements and cheque books to be ordered, as well as giving the balance on the account, and are known as 'dedicated ATM cards'. Second-generation ATM cards are multi-functional, being also debit cards and cheque guarantee cards. Both first and second generation ATM cards operate on a customer's bank account.

Credit cards also frequently permit cash withdrawals from ATMs but these, of course, operate on the credit card account and not the bank account.

We shall discuss ATM cards again later in the book, because they are now widely issued by building societies. In 2000, there were 24,170 bank ATMs (over 7,000 of which were located away from bank branches) plus well over 4,000 building society ATMs; 50m bank debit cards; and 50m bank credit cards. The statistics show that there is increasing demand for ATMs situated at supermarkets, motorway services and airports and increasing use of 'cash back' facilities offered by retailers.

ATM queries were, at first, the largest single type of complaint handled by the Banking Ombudsman, now the Financial Services Ombudsman (Banking and Loans) and PINs must never be revealed to third parties or written where they might be seen by anyone other than the customer. Revealing a PIN would constitute 'gross negligence' on the part of a customer.

It is widely acknowledged now that 'phantom withdrawals' are possible without customers being either dishonest or negligent. Numbers of ATM complaints to the Banking Ombudsman have fallen considerably in recent years, especially since the banks agreed to limit customer loss on card fraud to £50 (in line with credit cards) where cards are lost or stolen and the customer has not been negligent with the PIN.

Many debit cards in issue are also members of Europe-wide or worldwide networks such as MAESTRO and CIRRUS (both linked to Mastercard) to allow use overseas.

Banker's drafts

Banker's drafts are, in effect, cheques drawn by a bank branch on its head office. They have the advantage that payment cannot be stopped unless they are lost. The customer's account is usually debited with the value of the draft at the time it issued, plus any charges or, occasionally, cash will be paid in to the value of the draft and charges.

Drafts are used for legal transactions – especially for house completion payments (when the balance of the purchase price is paid) – although electronic transmission methods are superseding them, as we shall see later. They are also used for the purchase of cars, both new and second-hand. They are the nearest commercial bank product to a banknote – if they were payable to bearer and uncrossed they would to all intents and purposes be a banknote. However, they are always payable to order and crossed (see Chapter 10).

Building society cheques

These are an alternative to bankers' drafts. They cannot be stopped and so represent a guaranteed form of payment for people who do not have bank accounts. The depositor merely completes a withdrawal form, requesting a cheque rather than cash. The cheque can be made out either to the depositor or to the eventual payee. Occasionally, books of blank building society cheques have been stolen in transit from the printers, so that they are not as acceptable as a banker's draft.

Standing orders

These are a long-established bank product used for regular payments. The customer signs an authority requiring the bank to pay a stated sum on stated days (eg 1st of every month, 2nd of every January) to a named branch for the credit of a named customer of that branch. The sort code of this branch must be quoted also, together with the customer's account number. Usually, a reference number must be quoted so that the beneficiaries can credit their books of account with the sum received from the person who has signed the order. Until the mid-1980s standing orders were not permitted on deposit or savings accounts but they can now be accepted on some – such as the Flexible Savings Account of Lloyds Bank.

Frequently the beneficiary, who may be a large firm or organization such as the Automobile Association or Readers Digest, prints its own standing order forms which are then sent to its members, readers or customers. In this way the beneficiary knows that it will be able to trace all the incoming payments because they will bear its reference number.

Sometimes the customer has to send the standing order back to the beneficiary so that the reference number can be inserted before the beneficiary sends the order to the customer's branch.

The bank receiving the order has to take care to establish whether or not the amount to be paid changes from time to time and whether there is a date after which payments cease. Standing orders can be altered only by the customer, in writing.

Examples of regular payments where standing orders can be used include annual subscriptions, life assurance premiums, monthly and quarterly rents and mortgage repayments.

Direct debits

These are a development of the standing order. The difference is that they are originated (ie are placed in the banking system) by the beneficiary (the creditor) and not the debtor (the person owing the money). The banks introduced direct debits in the 1960s partly to stave off competition from the National Giro – now Girobank Plc.

Customers complete a 'direct debit mandate' which acts as an instruction to the branch where they keep their current account. The bank then agrees to accept the mandate and records the direct debit in its records. The mandate then goes to the beneficiary who records it so that the entries can be generated for the stated days.

Direct debits have several advantages:

- The beneficiary is aware of every transaction so that there are no 'unapplied credits' that cannot be traced.

- Most debits are paid by customers' banks with only a small minority being returned for lack of funds.

- Changes of tax rates – as with life assurance premiums for polices issued before March 1984 – can be easily recorded by the beneficiary.

- If the debit is for a variable amount, and many are, the amount can be increased in line with rising costs.

Safeguards are built into the system to prevent people initiating direct debits that are unauthorized or for excessive amounts. All originators must be approved by their bank and must give an indemnity to reimburse the customer and his or her bank for incorrect debits, eg where a computer tape or disk is accidentally processed twice. A further safeguard is that every originator must give adequate notice to customers of a forthcoming change in the amount of a direct debit. At present this is 14 days.

The disadvantages arise mostly with variable-amount direct debits. Some customers do not check their statements regularly and so may be unaware of rising subscription rates. If they had to change a standing order they would be alerted to increases and, moreover, might cancel their subscription. This disadvantage from the customers' stand-point is, of course, an advantage to the originating organizations.

Some customers refuse to sign direct debits, regarding them as impositions – allowing somebody to dip their hands, so to speak, in customers' pockets. However, they forget that they are enjoying a service or benefit from the originators of the direct debit and that this is only one of a number of methods of paying for the service.

Direct debits can be used for all payments suitable for standing orders but are unlikely to be used by small organizations such as the local tennis club or residents' association unless their bank sponsors them as a member of the direct debiting scheme. Such bodies must continue to rely on standing orders for their members' subscriptions.

Direct debits, as with standing orders, can be cancelled or amended by the customer writing to his or her branch. However, it is preferable to write to the originator and cancel a direct debit. Like standing orders, direct debits were originally not permitted on deposit or savings accounts but, since the mid-1980s, some banks have allowed them on certain of their deposit or savings accounts. However, there is still no uniform practice so each bank product must be scrutinized to see if standing orders and direct debits can be accepted.

This is also the case with credit cards where 'continuous payment authorities' can be authorized ie, direct debits as a credit card account.

In 2001 banks were encouraged to make transfer of direct debit data easier when customers transferred accounts between banks. This was part of the banks' response to the competition authorities focus on their 'monopoly' of payment mechanisms.

Bank giro credits (Credit Transfers)

This is a popular method of payment in much of Western Europe but has yet to find a wide audience in the UK. A person wishing to pay a sum of money to another person can, if he or she knows the details of the beneficiary's bank branch and account number, go into a branch of any bank and complete a form crediting the beneficiary's account with that sum. If the credit has to go to another bank or branch, the form used is a bank giro credit.

This seems very simple but one problem is that the form is sometimes incorrectly completed, so that it is impossible to trace the beneficiary. Customers and others are therefore strongly encouraged to use slips pre-printed by the bank or the beneficiary. Examples of these can be found at the foot of every gas, electricity and telephone bill, and some organizations, eg hire purchase companies and local authority rent departments, provide their borrowers and tenants with pre-printed books of bank giro credits.

The banks process the transactions, as we shall see later, and subsequently credit the beneficiary's account. However, the beneficiaries may not be advised of the receipt until they read their statements because the receiving bank assumes that the advice was sent by the person making the payment. Even if this is the case, the advice notice does not always specify the date on which payment will be made.

Credits transferred electronically are a major part of Internet and direct banking. Payment details of regular bills are held by the bank and customers trigger these, often adding the amount to be paid via an Internet or telephone connection with the bank.

A development of the bank giro system, using electronic methods of funds transfer, is BACS (see below). It is available to large organizations with their own computers.

Credit cards

Credit cards were introduced into the UK in 1966, when Barclays launched its Barclaycard, using computer systems developed by the Bank of America. In 1972 the Access credit card was launched by the Joint Credit Card Company (JCCC) owned by Lloyds, Midland and National Westminster banks. Since then, Access cards have been offered by Royal Bank of Scotland and Bank of Ireland.

Access was restrictive in its membership policy, being the sole UK representative of the Mastercard network, based in the USA. However, the rival network, VISA, which includes Barclaycard, has been more open in its attitude to new entrants. VISA now includes cards issued by smaller banks and, recently, by building societies.

The division between Barclays, part of VISA, and the other big three banks, part of Mastercard, has ended. Lloyds, Midland and National Westminster have joined VISA while Barclays and TSB have joined Mastercard. In July 1989, the JCCC adopted the name 'Signet' to establish a distinctive image in a climate of increasingly cut-throat competition. Because its shareholders have now joined VISA, Signet was trying to avoid becoming largely a data-processing organization but has now ceased operations, and the brand 'Access' is no more.

Credit card issuers derive their income from two sources:

a) commission charged to retailers and others such as hotels and insurance brokers, who accept the card in payment of sales (up to 5% of revenue); and

b) interest charged to cardholders who do not repay all their balance within 25 days of the date shown on their monthly statement.

Each merchant – the technical name for a retailer or outlet – and cardholder is given a limit. For instance, merchants may have a limit of £50 per transaction beyond which they cannot accept a card without authorization by the card issuer. This is normally done on-line but can be by phone call. Cardholders have higher limits, eg £2500, which their total balance at any one time must not exceed.

With each statement, cardholders are given a wide range of

repayment options, from repaying the whole balance to repaying only 5% of it, or in full if the balance is £5 or less. It is entirely up to the cardholders how much they repay, provided that it is between the maximum and the minimum. This illustrates how flexible a method of payment and repayment a credit card can be. The traditional minimum repayment is 5% but it was raised briefly by the government to 15% in 1973 during a severe credit squeeze. Interest is charged monthly on the outstanding balance, should the amount not be repaid in full. It is calculated from the date of each transaction.

You should note that the bank card companies use the term 'cardholder' rather than 'customer' to avoid the possibility of being estopped (prevented in law) from denying that a banker/customer relationship exists (see Chapter 7).

Most credit cards can be used in ATMs but there is an immediate fee or interest charge, much the same as with a cash advance on a credit card over a bank counter.

Affinity cards are credit cards linked to a charity or an organization such as the AA or RAC. This can also be linked to a lifestyle such as the Arts Card, which can be associated with one of nearly 50 orchestras, theatres and other organizations connected with the performing arts, chosen by the cardholder. Cards associated with football clubs are also used. The chosen organization receives a cash sum from the bank for each cardholder that chooses it, payable when the Arts Card is first used, and a percentage of the transactions for which the card is used.

Until 1990, no enrolment or annual fees were charged to cardholders. In February 1990, Lloyds Bank began to charge its Access cardholder £12 per annum, although this was linked to a reduction in interest from 2.2% to 1.9% a month. Other banks followed, but not all did so.

By the early 1990s, it seemed that credit cards were a product that had reached the decline stage of its product life cycle (PLC to marketeers – with four stages: introduction, growth, maturity and decline). Debit cards seemed poised to sweep the field, and the annual fees indicated that pricing policy was to 'squeeze' the product out of existence. However, this has not occurred. Also, there have been further developments. Better credit-scoring procedures, low interest rates (1997 onwards) and an economy growing via consumer confidence have combined to make credit cards very popular. Other incentives include:

- add-ons, such as air-miles whereby more usage of the card can entitle the holder to a free airline flight.

- co-branding of cards. The leading example is the GM card, issued by Beneficial Bank, whereby card-holders can obtain a reduction in the price of a new Vauxhall car of up to £2,500 from their spending with the card over a period of 5 years. [GM stands for General Motors Inc who are the American owners of Vauxhall]. Ford and Peugeot have similar cards co-branded with other banks.

- licence cards, for which the artwork and name are purchased from, say, a pop-star under licence. The first such card in the UK is the Star Trek card issued by the Bank of Scotland. In the USA, the Rolling Stones credit card, with the famous tongue logo, has resulted in more than 50,000 applications. In 1996, Beneficial Bank began issuing licence cards, following from its experience with affinity cards and the co-branded GM card.

- Low- or fixed-interest offers on balances transferred from other credit cards. Often these are fixed for a year.

Figure 9
Bank plastic cards 1987 – 2000 (000's)

	1987	*1992*	*2000*
No. of credit cards	24,476	26,476	49,705
No. of debit cards	n/a	22,596	49,729
No. of cheque cards*	28,446	42,590	56,604
Credit cards:			
No. of transactions (millions)	522	715	1,542
Value of transactions (£millions)	16,613	31,272	95,169
Debit Cards:**			
No of transactions (millions)	n/a	522	2,337
Value of transactions (£millions)	n/a	13,840	75,987
Card Fraud: (£millions)			
Cheque Card (to 1989)	25.9	n/a	n/a
Cheque Guarantee Card (from 1990)	n/a	25.6	9.0
Credit Card	n/a	76.7	163.8
Debit Card	n/a	43.9	86.1
Other	n/a	18.8	32.9
TOTAL FRAUD:	25.9	165.0	292.6

* Includes Barclaycards which are also counted as Visa credit cards.
** Covers UK domestic transactions only.

Source: British Bankers' Association / APACS.

Smart cards

Smart cards or 'The Electronic Purse' were pioneered in the UK by MONDEX (A consortium of Midland Bank, NatWest Bank and BT). Smart cards have yet to gain national coverage although extensive pilot schemes have taken place, notably in Swindon.

The smart card is a multi-function plastic card based around a computerized memory chip embedded in the card. It uses a technology different to the traditional magnetic strip cards and so the spread of smart cards will depend on retailers obtaining appropriate point-of-sale (POS) equipment.

The functions of the MONDEX card comprise:

- Debit card

- ATM withdrawal

- Card-to-card transfers (without passing through the bank accounts)

- 'Store' of credit for small transactions

- Multi-currency facility

- Greater security in addition to PIN

- Store of personal information/record of transactions

- Use for Internet shopping

Although MONDEX is expected to be expensive for banks and customers initially, it does represent the industry's best chance of reducing cash-handling costs in the future. The 21 billion cash transactions of under £10 in 1997 are the prime target for MONDEX.

The Euro

Although the UK decided not to join the Single European Currency (Euro) when it was launched on 1 January 2002, UK banks did need to gear up to accept the currency. Retailers in the south of England, London, the Channel Islands and at airports began to accept Euros, giving change in sterling. Accordingly UK banks need to ensure that Euro deposit or conversion services are available at reasonable rates for these retail customers. Customers invoicing in Euros for export also need to be catered for. For customers wishing to travel to a Eurozone country Euronotes can be provided (see below).

Store cards

Store cards are a type of credit card but they are issued by stores rather than by banks. For customers, they have two disadvantages: they can usually be used only in selected stores and their interest rates are higher than those charged by VISA and Access. An advantage is that cardholders can receive discounts on purchases and visit previews of sales. For example, occasional late-night receptions or pre-Christmas sales events can be held for cardholders.

From the store's viewpoint their advantages are that their cardholders constitute a known customer base, to whom they can send details of sales and special offers, and that they do not have to pay commission to VISA and Access. To some extent the stores must charge higher interest rates because of the absence of any 'merchants' commission', as it is called. A disadvantage can arise if the average transaction is too small. Boots, for example, withdrew its charge card in 1988 mainly because the processing costs of numerous small transactions were more than the interest received on the outstanding balances.

Marks & Spencer's Chargecard is probably the best known storecard. It now has a large cardholder base of well over 3 million, and it has used this base to launch its own unit trust. Personal loans are also available and a pension scheme and life insurance have been introduced. There is also a budget account with a credit limit of 25 times the monthly payment by the cardholder.

Credit cards, along with all forms of 'plastic money', are the fastest-changing part of banking and finance – further changes can be expected every year.

Charge cards

Charge cards – American Express and Diners Club – are slightly different to credit cards. They charge no interest, have no limit for card holders, except that all balances on the monthly statement must be fully repaid within 25 days, and charge an enrolment fee to cardholders – or members as American Express terms them. Advertisements remind us that 'membership has its privileges' usually in hotel and airline reservations. The absence of any limit is also an advantage, particularly when overseas travel is involved.

International means of payment

These would form a whole chapter of more specialist books, because they are so numerous, but here we can briefly mention several used by personal customers of banks.

Traveller's cheques

These were an American product but are now used worldwide. The customer purchases these cheques, from a bank or travel agent, and then signs them in the presence of the cashier, the cost usually being debited to the customer's current account or paid in cash (or added to the cost of the holiday). Later, when abroad or in the UK, the customer can cash them at a bank, hotel, or large shop by signing them again, with the clerk or shop assistant checking that the two signatures are similar. Moreover, proof of identity is often required, such as the customer's passport.

In the UK the traveller's cheques market is dominated by Thomas Cook. In banking terms the business is very lucrative because the bank holds the buyers' money until the traveller's cheque is encashed and presented. This can take weeks or even months, during which time the bank has free use of the customer's money.

Foreign currency

Foreign currency can be bought in the UK. Usually the major currencies required by the UK holidaymakers going abroad can be supplied by banks on demand because the branch maintains a bureau de change (sometimes called a foreign currency till), but occasionally there may be two or three days' delay while the currency is ordered. A commission is often made for this service, which may be free to holders of certain types of accounts.

This service is also available through some travel agents and at the Post Office as well as independent bureaux de change in larger cities.

Travellers can also use credit cards and ATM cards abroad, as mentioned earlier.

Telegraphic and mail transfers

For larger amounts normally associated with trading the payment can be made by telegraphic transfer (TT) or mail transfer (MT). As with a bank giro credit, full details such as bank account number and invoice number must be provided on the application form so that the payment can be applied to the beneficiary's account at the bank in the foreign country. For some of these transfers the UK bank may use a computer-based message system called SWIFT.

Banker's drafts

For larger payments, eg the deposit on the purchase of a house overseas, a banker's draft can be used. The UK branch will draw a draft, usually in the overseas currency, on a foreign correspondent bank near to the property being purchased. The UK will, of course, immediately advise its foreign correspondent of its action, so that the necessary bookkeeping can be done.

Summary

People can choose to pay their debts in many ways: cash, cheques, debit cards, ATM cards, banker's drafts, building society cheques, postal orders, standing orders, direct debits, bank giro credits, credit cards, store cards or charge cards. Additionally, payments may be made by traveller's cheques, foreign currency, or telegraphic transfer.

- Cash is suitable for small amounts.

- Cheques often need to be backed by a cheque guarantee card.

- Debit cards are relatively new, and should become even more popular, especially when their functionality is improved with the 'Electronic Purse'.

- Banker's drafts and building society cheques are used when the buyer takes possession immediately, as with a house or car.

- Standing orders help the customer to make regular fixed payments.

- Direct debits are better for variable payments.

- Bank giro credits, like standing orders, need to have full details of the transaction written or encoded on them.

- Internet or Direct banks offer electronic bank giro credits.

- Credit cards are changing considerably.

- Charge cards give the holder no credit but greater spending power.

- Store cards are still a threat to bank credit cards.

Further Reading – Chapter 9

Annual Abstract of Banking Statistics, British Bankers Association.
Arora A, (1992), *Electronic Banking & The Law*, Banking Technology.
Gandy A and Chapman C, (1996), *The Electronic Bank*, CIB Books.
Website: http://www.apacs.org.uk

10 Funds transfer: cheques and the clearing systems

Objectives

After studying this chapter you should be able to:

- [ ] State the legal definition of a cheque.

- [ ] Explain what a bill of exchange is.

- [ ] Describe the various payment systems operating in the UK.

- [ ] Describe the changes in cheque clearing brought about by truncation.

- [ ] Trace the growth of automated and electronic systems and the expected decline of paper-based systems.

- [ ] State the requirements for entry to the automated and high-value systems.

- [ ] Explain what is meant by 'negotiability'.

What is a cheque?

With, on average, 8 million cheques being written every working day, cheques are still a very important part of our payment system.

But remember, they are not money, only a means of transferring money.

In the last chapter we briefly defined a cheque. The detailed legal definition of a cheque comes from the Bills of Exchange Act 1882.

> *A cheque is an unconditional order in writing, addressed by one person to a banker, signed by the person giving it, requiring the banker to pay on demand, or at a fixed or determinable future date, a sum certain in money, to a specified person or to the order of a specified person or to bearer.*

The definition is based closely on the definition of a Bill of Exchange, except that a cheque is payable on demand and drawn on a banker.

We must examine the various sections of the definition.

An unconditional order
There should be no conditions which must first be fulfilled, such as 'on the arrival at Southampton of the Queen Elizabeth II pay...' or 'if my account can stand it, pay...'.

To a banker
A banker is defined in the Bills of Exchange Act 1882 as a person carrying on a banking business, which is not a very helpful definition. However, we now have a definition from the Banking Act 1987, as we saw in Chapter 6.

In writing and signed
The writing must be permanent and readable and must include the signature of the person giving the order. Although we are now in an age of electronics, cheques are paper-based which means that electronic coding by itself cannot yet create a legal cheque. (However, cheques do not have to be written on paper.)

To pay on demand or at a fixed or determinable future date
This date must be able to be calculated exactly. Thus, a post-dated cheque is, in theory, acceptable. Banks frown on the deliberate post-

dating of cheques, however, because they can inadvertently pay a cheque before the due date because of the curtailed checking procedures they now adopt.

A sum certain in money

Usually sterling is the money but, as we shall see later, there are foreign currency clearings in London too. Also, it is not possible for a cheque to be for '£30,000 plus interest from 1 January 2002' because this is an uncertain amount.

To or to the order of a specified person, or to bearer

The person must be named; fictitious names invalidate the cheque.

'Petty Cash', 'Cash' or 'Wages' are not persons and cheques made out in this way are not, strictly, cheques but, merely, mandates addressed to the banker. However, a cheque can be made to 'bearer', although it can be risky to do this if the cheque is subsequently stolen or lost because the finder – now the 'bearer' – can have the cheque collected.

Bills of exchange

If that legal jargon is too complicated, then we can try to be more down to earth. A cheque is an example of a bill of exchange, and so we shall begin with a description of a bill of exchange.

A bill of exchange is a definite order in writing by one person to a second person to pay a precise sum of money to that first person, or to a third person or to bearer at or after a precise date.

Usually, the second person, to whom the bill is addressed, owes money to the first person, or the drawer of the bill. The drawer is a creditor of the person (the debtor) and instructs the debtor to pay the drawer or somebody to whom the drawer owes money.

We can show this as a series of steps in a situation in which bills of exchange are often used.

Step 1   Drawer has exported goods to a foreign importer (drawer's debtor).

Step 2   Drawer needs to be paid by his debtor for the goods.

Step 3   Drawer writes out (draws) a bill of exchange on the importer (debtor).

Step 4   Drawer sends the bill of exchange to the importer (debtor), who acknowledges the debt by signing across the front of the bill – accepting it, as this is called.

An acceptance can be for a payment at a future date, eg three months' time, or for immediate payment – at sight.

Step 5   If the bill is a sight bill, the acceptor should pay the drawer or the other person named on the bill immediately, perhaps by one of the methods described at the end of the last chapter.

Step 6   If the bill is not a sight bill then the acceptor returns it to the drawer, who can either file it until nearer the date of payment, and then post it to the acceptor for payment or sell the bill to a discount house or bank, for an amount somewhat less than its face value so as to get immediate payment.

This difference in the two amounts is known as the discount on the bill, as we noticed in Chapter 5.

Bills of Exchange are becoming rarer in UK and in foreign trade as more secure methods of payment are developed.

Back to cheques

With a cheque the debtor is usually the bank, ie when the customer's account is in credit. The steps then become:

Step 1   The drawer of the cheque has deposited money with the bank, which becomes his debtor.

Step 2   The drawer needs some cash, or to pay someone else (his creditor).

Step 3   The drawer writes out (draws) a cheque on the bank –

the drawee or paying bank (the debtor).

Step 4   Either the drawer takes the cheque to the bank branch on which it is drawn, which 'pays' the cheque and hands over cash or the drawer sends the cheque to his creditor (the payee) who sends it via his bank and the clearing to the drawee bank.

When the customer's account is in debit, he or she is the bank's debtor, because he or she owes it money.

The traditional clearings

The traditional paper clearings refer to the well-known three-day clearing cycle during which time the funds represented by cheques are transferred from the drawers' accounts to the payees. When the creditor (payee) receives the cheque, he or she takes it to his or her bank (known as the collecting bank) which scrutinizes it and stamps it with its crossing stamp. Then begin three hectic days.

On the first day the cheque is at the collecting bank. That night it is sent by road to London.

It is transferred from one head office to another on the second day; that night it used to be sent by road to the paying bank but nowadays Paying Bank Truncation (PBT) allows only electronic messages to pass to the paying bank branch.

On the third day, or on the morning of the fourth, the paying bank should decide whether or not to pay the cheque. The 'days' are working days, so that weekends and public holidays such as Christmas and Easter can intervene and extend the process a bit. Also on the third day the banks settle their net indebtedness by making transfers between their own accounts held at the Bank of England. If a bank is a net collector of cheques (for example, a bank with a large number of retailers as account holders) it may find that the other banks pay funds to it on a daily basis.

On the fourth day the collecting bank can either assume that the cheque has been paid or it receives a message to indicate that it remains unpaid. At this time the collecting bank must reverse the credit on the payee's account and notify its customer (payee) that the cheque is unpaid. Eventually, via the post, the cheque itself is returned to the collecting branch for onward transmission to the payee.

Over the last 20 years the banks have recognized that the transmission of paper cheques, by road, the length and breadth of the country is a very costly exercise. Some banks have centralized processing capacity or outsourced it completely to gain efficiencies but it was not until the introduction of the Inter Bank Data Exchange (IBDE) and a change in the law in 1996 that the potential to stem this tide of paper was available (See section on truncation later).

In the 1980s, some fairly important changes occurred in the organization of both the UK debit and credit clearings. These are now run by three separate limited companies, co-ordinated by APACS, the Association for Payment Clearing Services.

Figure 10
The three day clearing cycle

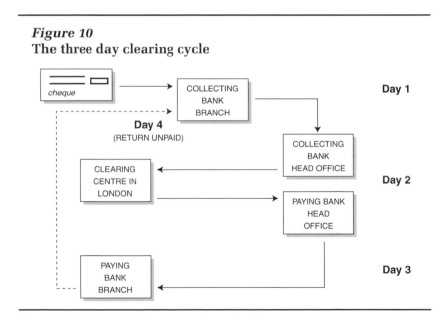

APACS

This is an association comprising:

1. Cheque and Credit Clearing Co Ltd which provides bulk debit clearings for England and Wales. There are separate cheque and credit clearings for Scotland and Northern Ireland.

2. CHAPS and Town Clearing Co Ltd which provides a high value, electronic credit clearing for the UK and, until February 1995, a high value paper debit clearing for the City of London.

3. BACS Ltd which provides bulk electronic credit and debit clearings for the UK.

Membership of each of these three clearing companies is open to any institution which, among other things, is:

*   adequately supervised for prudential purposes, ie normally a bank or building society;

*   providing business at a level at least equal to a minimum percentage – currently 0.5% – of the volume of that particular clearing.

Membership of a clearing gives full membership of APACS, but not necessarily of other clearings.

The full members of APACS in 2001 were the central bank, 11 commercial banks and one building society. In addition, 11 foreign banks were members of the CHAPS clearings only. There are also 'operational groupings' covering

a) City Markets and Corporate Payments

b) Card Payments,

c) Cash Services,

d) Electronic Commerce, and

e) Currency Clearings.

Also, there are associate members which link into one or more clearings via agency arrangements with full members.

Cheque and Credit Clearing Co Ltd

This operates the cheque clearing, until recently known as the general clearing, and the credit clearing between member banks and member building societies. We outlined the cheque clearing earlier in this chapter and the credit clearing operates to a similar time scale.

Comparable clearings operate within each member bank – the inter-branch clearings.

In 2000, 2,212 million cheques were handled by the cheque clearing. that is 8.6 million cheques for every working day of the year! This figure has more than doubled since 1972, but is now falling. Credit items cleared grew only slowly after 1980, and are now falling, partly due to substantial rises in the electronic credit clearing operated by BACS Ltd.

Settlement between full members is effected through their operational accounts at the Bank of England on the day – on the third working day of the cycle – when the paper items involved reach their destinations – the paying banks for cheques and the beneficiary banks for credits. That is the day when the amounts credited by the collecting banks become cleared funds and when interest is allowed on the amounts.

The Cheque and Credit Clearing Co Ltd works continually to improve the efficiency and quality of the clearings, laying down agreed formats for cheques and credits to allow them to be processed more effectively. In 2001 the company reported that it was working towards full collecting Bank Truncation (CBT -see later).

CHAPS Clearing Co Ltd

This was set up in 1984 and at first operated two distinct high value clearings:

Town Clearing

This involved between about 90 branches of member banks within a half-mile radius of the Bank of England. These branches closed for business at 3pm, not 3.30pm or later, and all cheques for sums of £100,000 and over that had been drawn on other 'Town Clearing' branches were sent by messenger to the Clearing House in Lombard Street that afternoon and either paid or returned by the paying bank later the same day. The average amount of a Town Clearing cheque was £2.6m in 1988, very much higher than an average item in the cheque clearing, which was £443.

The minimum amount of the Town Clearing was only raised in November 1989 from £10,000, at which level it had been since 1980. In February 1995 the Town Clearing ceased, and all items were moved to CHAPS or the general clearing.

CHAPS

This stands for Clearing House Automated Payment System. This provides single, high-value, same-day credit transfers by terminals located in bank branches throughout the UK. It was launched in 1984, with a view to replacing the Town Clearing but has since become nationwide in its coverage following the abolition of a minimum amount for an item. Demand was kept within reasonable bounds by the imposition of a £15 charge. In 1988, the average value of an item – strictly a CHAPS message – was about £1.9m with the 5.8m messages transmitted having a total value of £11.3 trillion (million million). In 1997, the figures were £2.0m; 17m messages and a total value of £36.4 trillion.

Instructions from customers for banks to issue CHAPS payment messages can be made:

- in writing;
- by telephone;
- by telex;
- by terminal or mainframe computer line;

- via a SWIFT terminal. (SWIFT is described later, because it deals with international messages between banks in many countries).

CHAPS will reduce the number of sterling bankers' drafts being issued because there is no risk of loss, the paper does not have to be sent physically to the collecting bank and, of course, the funds are 'cleared'. With a draft, although there is no risk of dishonour, the item does have to go through the clearing and hence value cannot be given on the day that the draft is paid into the payee's account.

There is no central processing CHAPS unit, just links between banks and their branches. Once a receiving branch has acknowledged receipt of a CHAPS message, the payment is irrevocable. Settlement between members takes place via the operating accounts at the Bank of England on the same day as the messages are transmitted. Cut-off time is now 3.10pm.

CHAPS accounts for 0.3% of APACS volumes and 92% of the total value of APACS clearings. Since 1999 APACS has offered a CHAPS service denominated in Euros. This has grown significantly and now handles volumes of 8,000 daily with an average daily value of €100m.

CHAPS is also working towards enlarging its membership (at a £100,000 annual fee) to other banks currently using CHAPS via intermediaries.

BACS Ltd

This was for some time called Bankers' Automated Clearing Services Ltd and, before that, the Inter-Bank Computer Bureau. Since 1985, it has been just BACS – pronounced 'bax'.

Working on a three-day cycle, BACS accepts items on disks, tapes and telecommunication links from either customers or the members themselves. It processes the standing orders and direct debits, which we described in the last chapter, as well as salaries, wages, pensions and bought ledger payments originating from the customers' own computers. The cycle is as follows:

Working day 1 (or earlier) Data is received by BACS at its Edgware centre in North West London for processing and despatch to the members.

Working day 2   Data is processed by the members, who advise the Bank of England of the necessary settlements to be made between them on their operational accounts with the Bank on the next working day.

Working day 3   Debit and credit entries are made on the customers' accounts and on the members' operational accounts at the Bank of England. The credits are thus 'cleared funds' when they reach the beneficiaries' bank accounts.

Unlike bank giro credits, which are paper-based, the originators' accounts under BACS are not debited two working days before the credit entries are made. This saving in interest for the originator is an advantage that helps to offset the extra cost which must be paid for using BACS. An advantage for the beneficiary is that the narrative or description of the credit on the statement gives the name of the payer, unlike a paper-based bank giro credit.

Direct debit originators are carefully vetted by their sponsoring banks before BACS facilities can be granted. Repayments for wrongful debits must be guaranteed by originators and so only the most creditworthy can apply.

BACS volumes grew to 3.3 billion items in 2000 – twice the volume in 1990.

BACS invested heavily in 2000 in updated technology and launched an automated direct debit instruction Service (AUDDIS). The company also advertised heavily to encourage use of direct debits.

At the end of 2001 BACS introduced the automatic transfer of direct debit instructions between members when customers transfer accounts. This is said to reduce transfer delays from six to four weeks and is designed to improve competition between account providers.

Figure 11
Clearing statistics 1987 – 2000 (000's) (London)

	1987	1992	2000
Cheque Clearing			
Inter Bank	2,060,708	2,173,888	1,704,068
Inter Branch	625,340	543,599	367,477
Credit Clearing			
Inter Bank	183,596	165,445	152,228
Inter Branch	257,448	259,064	204,176
BACS			
Direct Debits	485,864	1,000,574	2,009,670
Standing Orders	239,124	232,799	246,786
Direct Credits	346,246	586,174	1,059,751
Electronic Credits (inter branch)	76,352	67,851	64,820
CHAPS Sterling	4,387	9,079	21,705
Town Clearing*	4,638	125	n/a

* Town Clearing ceased in 1995

Source: British Bankers' Association.

The above clearing statistics show that the number of paper items is being eroded rapidly and that electronic means of payment are growing in volume. The value of electronic payments far outstrips paper too.

APACS 2001 forecasts show that these trends are likely to continue to the year 2010 as more plastic cards come into use and as ways are found to reduce the flow of paper.

APACS Operational groupings

City Markets Group and Corporate Payments

This group makes it possible for settlement banks to address developments and new initiatives across the spectrum of corporate electronic payments and city markets. It brings together APACS responsibilities for city markets and Securities Settlement Systems (SSS), treasurers' liquidity issues, electronic practices for international trade, Financial EDI and harmonizing utility bill payment by remote banking. The group is also responsible for providing a response to the Cruickshank Review findings that APACS structures prevented competition.

Card Payments Group

This comprises most of the APACS members, plus several associate members and many other organizations, including those that represent the shops and stores where the cards are used.

There are two main aspects – cheque guarantee cards and debit cards (including chip cards).

Members issue cards in an agreed standard format, with William Shakespeare's head as their hologram for cheque guarantee cards. Members may also use the symbol to identify the cheque guarantee function on a multi-purpose card – such as the Lloyds Bank Payment Card. The scheme seeks to ensure uniformity in order to facilitate the greater acceptability of the cards (remember, these are two of the qualities of money which we discussed in Chapter 2) and, just as important, to minimize fraud.

Current developments also cover e-cash, payment via the Internet, chip cards and the use of the PIN at retail outlets.

The card payments group is also responsible for fraud reduction measures and is working with merchants prone to the very prevalent Card Not Present (DNP) fraud such as mail order outlets to reduce risks.

Cash Services Group

This group has responsibility for liaison on issues of notes and coin, such as the introduction of the £2 coin and the phasing out of the old style 50p. It also has responsibility for issues concerning the Single European Currency.

Special presentations

Some cheques are not sent by the collecting bank through the clearing to the paying bank but are sent direct, usually by first-class post for faster presentation. Occasionally, the banks in a town may agree to allow special presentations by hand, across the counter of the paying bank.

The fate of the cheque will be decided a day earlier than if it had been sent through the cheque clearing. For this service the payee will be charged a fee by the collecting bank which will telephone the paying bank for 'advice of payment' – usually in the morning. Once a cheque is advised to the collecting bank as 'paid' the drawer cannot place a stop on it. To protect their customers and give them a chance to place a stop, some banks decline to answer such a telephone request until 3.30pm. Quite often, the drawer will be unaware of the special presentation, believing that the cheque will take three working days to be presented in the clearing and may have insufficient funds or have a cash flow problem.

Truncation

In May 1996 the Government laid an order before Parliament allowing for the removal of ' unnecessary and outdated' restrictions on banks, namely, the removal or amendment of Section 45 of the Bills of Exchange Act 1882. This was one of the recommendations of the National Consumer Council in 1983 and the Jack Committee in 1989. The Deregulation (Bills of Exchange) Order 1996 was passed following the Government's support for cheque truncation to be allowed. Jack recognized the need to retain customer rights in cases of fraud or forgery but said little about how banks could engineer this. Banks can now debit cheques to customers' accounts without the need to physically present them to the branch on which they were drawn.

Cheque truncation is not new, the technology is well tried and tested in Europe and operates in respect of Eurocheques too. In the UK banks have, for many years, 'truncated' cheques drawn on other branches of their own bank where these have been drawn under a cheque card or 'credit open' facility (strictly speaking these instruments are not 'cheques').

What is cheque truncation?

The essence of cheque truncation is the capture of the vital coded data on a cheque and the electronic transmission of that information in order to obtain payment. APACS suggests that with the enabling legislation in place it will take banks years to move towards full truncation. Currently truncation is by Paying Bank only (PBT), not by Collecting Bank. The Collecting Bank collates and sends cheques, via the Clearing House, to the Head Office of the Paying Bank between days one and two of the clearing cycle. Truncation takes place at the Head Office with the Paying Branch receiving only an electronic message on day three of the cycle. The branch of the bank on which the cheque is drawn may never see the physical cheque itself although future advances in Image Processing may allow selective viewing via computer link and IBDE.

Thus, banks are ready to dispense with the final part of the physical transmission process and plan to allow Collecting Bank Truncation (CBT) in the future. CBT could also give the opportunity to reduce the length of the clearing cycle as electronic messages could, in theory, be transmitted to paying branch direct from collecting branch on day two of the clearing cycle.

While APACS remains committed to CBT it notes that volumes of cheques are falling and agreement has yet to be reached between member banks on image processing, exchange and archival.

Negotiable instruments

The idea of negotiability developed from the custom of traders which became known as the law merchant, and the law of negotiability was codified by the Bills of Exchange Act 1882. At that time, the principal negotiable instrument was the bill of exchange but the Act also contains sections dealing with what was then a new negotiable instrument – the cheque, a bill of exchange drawn on a banker.

Since then, cheques have become very common but are no longer frequently transferred from person to person, so that they are tending to lose the characteristics of negotiability. This process was accelerated by the Cheques Act 1992, which we shall study in the next chapter. This Act strips all cheques with an 'A/c Payee' crossing (and they are now printed with this on them) of all the characteristics of negotiability. Such cheques are not transferable.

Negotiability

Negotiability is the characteristic possessed by a commercial or financial instrument, such as a cheque or banknote, where:

1. Transfer of ownership occurs:

    a) by delivery, if payable to bearer, such as a banknote, or

    b) by endorsement and delivery, if payable to order, such as a bill of exchange (see Chapter 11).

Most cheques are 'order' cheques, ie the payee has to order the drawee bank to pay somebody else, if the cheque is not being paid into the payee's account. This order is contained in the endorsement, which can be to a particular person or even to that person 'only'.

Some cheques are printed 'Pay... or Bearer'. These do not require endorsement because title to a bearer cheque passes by delivery alone.

2. The transferee (new owner) who takes the instrument:

    a) in good faith; and

    b) for value, ie not a gift;

    c) with no notice of any defect in the title (title means legal entitlement to ownership) of the transferor then obtains a legal title free of any equitable rights, eg the right of a previous holder who was tricked into transferring the bill to recover it, and may sue in his or her own name on the instrument.

3. No notice of the transfer need be given to the person originally liable on the instrument.

If I steal a £5 Bank of England note it is not mine. But if I buy some goods with it then the seller becomes the true owner of that note because he has fulfilled all three conditions in (2) above. Moreover, nobody has to tell the Bank of England who owns all their millions of notes.

However, if I steal a share certificate and then sell it, the purchaser does not have a valid title. Moreover, when most shares are bought and sold the new owner has to register his or her name with the company which issued the shares, a process which often leads to delays in obtaining a good title. The exceptions are bearer shares, where the title passes by mere delivery.

Today, bills of exchange are rare in domestic trade and cheques are commonplace. However, there are now a large number of newer varieties of negotiable instruments which, as well as bills of exchange, cheques and banknotes, include:

- Bearer bonds and debentures – including sterling commercial paper, first issued in 1986.

- Bearer shares.

- Treasury bills.

- American depository receipts (ADRs), which is how American shares are traded in London.

- Blank, signed share transfer forms.

- Signed allotment letters of shares newly issued.

- Bearer scrip.

- Dividend warrants.

- Interest warrants.

- Circular notes, floating rate notes, certificates of deposits (CDs).

Summary

- A cheque is a bill of exchange drawn on a banker. Usually the drawer is a creditor of the bank, which is therefore the debtor of the drawer. More technically, a cheque is 'an unconditional order in writing, addressed by one person to a banker, signed by the person giving it, requiring the banker to pay on demand, or at a fixed or determinable future time, a sum certain in money, to, or to the order of, a specified person or bearer'.

- A collecting bank acts for the payee of a cheque. The paying banker is the drawee bank whose name and address are printed on the cheque.

- The clearings in England and Wales, together with other payment systems, are controlled by APACS, which comprises separate organizations for:

  - The cheque and credit clearing;

  - CHAPS;

  - BACS.

- Special presentations are sent direct to the drawee bank and not via the clearing.

- With billions of cheques in the clearings, efforts are being made to reduce the numbers, by automation, by increasing the use of plastic cards and by truncation.

- Negotiability is that characteristic of those financial instruments where ownership is transferred by delivery, or endorsement and delivery and where, if the new owner takes the instrument in good faith, for value and with no notice of any defect in the title of the person transferring it to him, the new owner acquires a perfect legal title. No notice of any transfer need to be given to the person originally liable on the instrument.

Further Reading – Chapter 10

Annual Abstract of Banking Statistics, British Bankers' Association.
   Arora A, (1992), *Electronic Banking & The Law*, Banking Technology
   http://www.apacs.org.uk

11 The collecting bank and the paying bank

Objectives

After studying this chapter you should be able to:

☐ Define the terms collecting bank and paying bank.

☐ State their different functions and duties.

☐ Apply the statutory protections available to them.

☐ Describe the conditions under which this protection is granted.

☐ State the reasons why cheques are returned.

☐ Explain the procedure when cheques are stopped.

Introduction

Here we enter legal territory again, with two important Acts, a number of cases and several terms, such as collecting bank and paying bank, which banks still frequently use.

The collecting bank is the bank branch where a person (usually a customer of that branch but not necessarily) brings the cheque for credit to his or her account.

The paying bank is the branch whose name and address are

printed on the front of the cheque and whose bank branch number (technically known as the sort code) is encoded at the bottom of the cheque in magnetic ink. This encoding ensures that the cheque is automatically sorted correctly to reach that particular branch.

> *Note:* *This chapter is concerned with legal theory; in practice, checking is expensive for the paying bank, and so a greater burden is placed on the collecting bank, especially as a result of anti-money laundering procedures. That is why credits are usually examined thoroughly at the counter.*

The collecting bank: examining cheques

When the cheque is brought to the collecting bank, the staff there must examine it for a number of things.

Figure 12
Key parts of a cheque

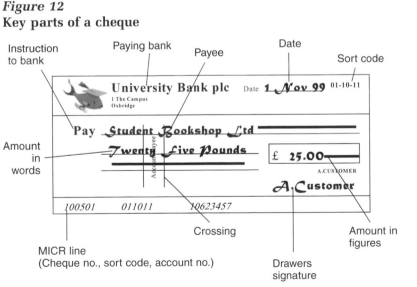

The date on the cheque

This must be:

1.   not more than six months earlier, eg on 1 May 2002, a cheque dated 31 October 2001 or earlier should not be accepted because the instruction may have lapsed;

2.   not post-dated, which means dated for a day which has yet to happen. Thus, on 1 June a collecting bank should not accept a cheque dated 4 June or later because that cheque will reach the paying bank on 3 June and so will be post-dated. The reason why post-dated cheques are unacceptable to banks is that the customer's instruction takes effect only on the date shown on the cheque. If the collecting bank does not reject the post-dated cheque then the paying bank will.

However, if there is no date on the cheque then the clerk can insert the day's date with a date stamp.

The amount

The amount in words on the cheque must be the same as the amount in figures. If they differ slightly then the collecting banks usually claim the lower and amend the credit slip if necessary to ensure that the entries balance. A pencil note will also be made on the cheque. For instance, if the words are 'One hundred and forty seven pounds' and the figures are '£147-47', then 47p will be deducted from the credit and 'We claim £147-00' will be written in pencil beneath the box for the amount in figures. However, if the discrepancy is more than a pound or two then the customer must be contacted by the collecting bank, with the cheque being deleted from the credit slip and returned to him or her. The customer will then contact the drawer for either the cheque to be altered or, preferably, a new cheque to be issued. According to the Bills of Exchange Act 1882 the amount in words is the definitive amount of the cheque.

Payee's name

The payee's name on the cheque must be the same as the name of the account to be credited. If not, then a procedure known as endorsement by the payee and perhaps by other people must be followed.

However, following the Cheques Act, 1992, it is probable that the collecting bank will require the cheque to be deleted from the credit, as we shall see later in this chapter.

The collecting banker should also be mindful of the relationship between the Payee and the drawer of the cheque to guard against possible fraud. In *Marquis of Bute v Barclays* (1955) cheques were collected payable to 'McGaw for Marquis of Bute', drawn on the Department of Agriculture. These should not have been collected for McGaw's personal account.

Endorsement

An endorsement is a signature on the back of a cheque, corresponding to the name of the payee shown on the front.

When is an endorsement required?

An endorsement is required whenever an order cheque (as opposed to a bearer cheque) is to be paid into the account of someone other than the named payee. Because the majority of cheques are, as a result of the Cheques Act 1992, non-transferable, transfers are becoming increasingly less frequent. The rules of endorsement do still apply to bills of exchange, to which the Cheques Act does not apply. One other exception is where a cheque has a large 'R' printed on the front, to the left of the box for the amount in figures; this indicates that there is a printed receipt form on the back which must be signed. Such receipts are sometimes used by assurance companies when paying sums due on policies or claimed under policies.

Types of endorsement

Endorsements are of three kinds – each example here relates to a bill of exchange payable to S Parrow:

1. Blank: S Parrow

2. Specific: Pay K Ite or order. S Parrow

3. Restrictive: Pay S E A Gull only. S Parrow

A specific endorsement requires the bill of exchange to be credited to the account of the person to whom it is endorsed or, if not, then his or her endorsement is also required. A restrictive endorsement restricts the transferability of the bill of exchange to the person named in the endorsement, in our example, S E A Gull.

The crossing

At its simplest, a crossing consists of two parallel lines on the front of a cheque, running at right angles across the lines for the name of the payee and the amount in words. These lines require the cheque to be paid to a bank or building society account and not to be cashed over the counter.

Strictly, crossings are instructions to the paying banker, but they can contain instructions to the collecting banker, as explained below.

Figure 13
Crossings on cheques

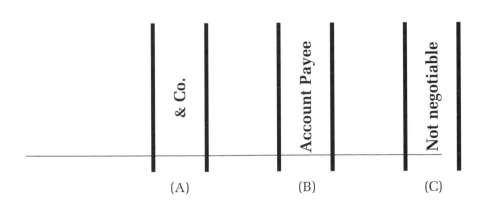

(A)   (B)   (C)

(A) General and Special crossings

Most crossings are general crossings. These are just the two parallel lines, although they often contain the inscription '& Co'. The inscription dates from the days in the last century when banks were partnerships and when the collecting bank had to insert the rest of its name, eg Coutts & Co.

Special crossings contain the name of a bank written between the two lines, like the Coutts & Co crossing in the previous paragraph. This crossing had been converted from a general crossing to a special crossing.

Many large companies and organizations cross-stamp all the cheques they receive immediately the envelopes are opened or when the cheques are accepted by their cashiers.

If a cheque has been cross-stamped by another bank or is crossed specially to another bank, then the collecting bank should return it to the customer and delete it from its credit slip. As we shall see later, if the collecting bank does not reject it now, then the paying banker will refuse to pay it and will return it to the collecting banker.

(B) Account Payee

This addition to a crossing is an instruction to the collecting bank to collect the cheque only for the credit of the payee's account. Often the words 'Account payee only' are used. This phrase was given statutory effect by the Cheques Act 1992. Section 1 of this Act amended the Bills of Exchange Act 1882 by inserting a new section into that Act (S.81A) which reads:

(1) Where a cheque is crossed and bears across its face the words 'account payee' or 'a/c payee', either with or without the word 'only', the cheque shall not be transferable, but shall only be valid as between the parties thereto.

Unless customers request otherwise, banks now only issue cheque books with the crossing 'Account Payee' already printed on them. This one Act, therefore, has made cheques non-negotiable.

In *Honorable Society of the Middle Temple v Lloyds Bank plc and Sekerbank* (1999) the negligent collection of an 'Account Payee' cheque by Lloyds Turkish agent made Lloyds liable for conversion too.

(C) Not negotiable

An important feature of many crossings is the addition of the phrase 'not negotiable' between the two parallel lines. This phrase does not restrict the cheque's transferability but it does mean that if the cheque is stolen then the thief or anybody to whom the thief later passes the cheque cannot become the true owner.

In *Great Western Railway Co Ltd v London & County Bank* (1901), the bank had been in the habit of cashing cheques for a local government official known as a Poor Law Overseer. The GWR had issued a cheque crossed 'not negotiable' for its poor law rates and the overseer had fraudulently acquired it and cashed it at the bank. The GWR sued the bank for conversion. It was held that because the cheque was now a non-negotiable instrument, the overseer had no right to the cheque and neither had the bank, which therefore had to repay the money to the GWR.

A 'not negotiable' crossing is, therefore, a great protection to the drawer, and helps to ensure that nobody takes the money away from the payee.

Alterations

All alterations to cheques must be signed by the drawer. These occur frequently with the date, the payee's name or the amount in words. In *Slingsby v District Bank* (1932) a fraudster added his name to that of the payee, materially altering the cheque. The court held that the cheque was invalid and should not have been collected. We look again at alterations when the paying bank position is reviewed.

Signature

Every cheque must have a signature. Unsigned cheques should not be accepted for collection.

Not mutilated

The cheque should not be torn in half or otherwise mutilated. If it is torn in any way, the customer should confirm that the tear is not across the whole cheque by making a mark in ink on the back of the cheque at the point where the tear ends. Otherwise the paying banker might return it marked 'mutilated cheque', because its customer may have intended to destroy it.

Each of these things which a collecting bank has to check for may seem daunting. How, for example, can it be certain that it is collecting each cheque for the true owner. The answer is: it cannot but, in most circumstances, it is protected by Act of Parliament.

Suspicious circumstances

Over the years cases have arisen where banks have been shown to be negligent in collecting cheques and have lost statutory protection.

In *Nu-Stilo Footwear v Lloyds* (1956) cheques were collected for an individual's account but had been made out to a Limited Company (and a forged endorsement added). The bank was negligent and liable in conversion because it had not questioned this transaction.

In *Thackwell v Barclays* (1986) the bank again lost protection because it should have known that the endorsements on two large cheques were forged. The bank lost no money, however, because the courts would not allow the true owner (who had obtained the cheques by deception) to succeed.

Collecting banks should, therefore, look out for any account activity that is out of keeping with the account to be credited.

Statutory protection for the collecting banker

This is provided by section 4 of the Cheques Act 1957, which states that the collecting bank shall incur no liability to the true owner where its customer was not the true owner. This protection is subject to three restrictions:

1. The collecting bank is acting for a customer.

2. The collecting bank acts in good faith.

3. The collecting bank acts without negligence.

As we saw in *Ladbroke v Todd* and *Lloyds Bank v E B Savory & Co* (Chapter 8), a bank can act negligently and so lose the statutory protection, but in *Marfani & Co Ltd v Midland Bank* the bank retained the protection of the Act. A bank collecting a stolen cheque crossed 'A/c payee only' would also lose this protection.

The paying banker

The paying bank has legal obligations to its customer (who has drawn the cheque). The bank must pay the cheque if:

- the balance of an account is in credit or the limit on an overdrawn account permits it;

- the cheque is technically in order;

- there is no legal bar to payment, such as death, bankruptcy or mental incapacity of the customer; no garnishee order, or criminal confiscation order or Mareva injunction (see later in this chapter);

- there is no stop placed on the cheque by the customer;

- the cheque was properly issued in conjunction with a cheque guarantee card;

The paying banker must not pay the cheque if:

- the customer has placed a stop on it;

- the bank has notice of a defect in the payee's title;

- the drawer's signature is forged.

The paying banker has discretion to pay or not to pay the cheque if the balance so created would be slightly above any agreed limit on an overdrawn account.

Time limits for decisions

House cheques
These are where the collecting bank is also the paying bank. The banker has to take decisions within certain time limits. Thus, if an uncrossed cheque is presented at the counter of the branch on which it has been drawn (a house cheque) for encashment by the presenter the immediate action is necessary.

Similarly, an immediate decision is required when a crossed cheque drawn on that branch is paid in at that branch, for credit to an account at the branch or for credit of another account at a different branch or bank through the credit clearing.

Special presentations

When a cheque is presented specially by the collecting banker, the paying banker may be able to postpone a decision by a few hours. If the presentation is by post, a decision is required on the day of the receipt. Usually, the collecting banker will telephone to find out whether the cheque has been paid or not. Once the paying banker has informed the collecting banker that the cheque is paid then the customer cannot put a stop on it. Accordingly, some banks decline to give a decision until the close of business, in order to protect their customers.

If the presentation is by hand, usually ten minutes is sufficient for the necessary enquiries to be made as to the balance and existence of any countermand (stop). The messenger from the collecting bank will then be handed a banker's payment for the amount of the special presentation. For small amounts, a credit will be sent in the credit clearing.

Through the cheque clearing

The cheque must be paid or returned on the day it was received by the paying banker or up to 12 noon on the following business day (but only in cases of 'inadvertence'). If it is returned on the latter day and the cheque exceeds £100, the collecting banker must be informed by telephone.

Examining the cheque: the paying banker

Examination should take place of the following places: first, the front of the cheque; second, the back of the cheque and; third, elsewhere in the paying bank against its records.

1. The front of the cheque

Here a good guide is to start with the date at the top right-hand corner and go around the cheque in a clockwise direction.

a) *Date* As discussed at the beginning of this chapter, the date must not be older than six months' previously and not post-dated. The date can be inserted if there isn't one.

b) *Amount in figures* This must agree with the amount in words.

c) *Signature* This must be that of the customer to whose account it will be debited and must not be forged. If necessary, reference must be made to the file of customers' signature cards to verify the signature (see below).

d) *Amount in words* This must agree with the amount in figures. The amount in words is the correct amount of the cheque, the figures are not part of the contract.

c) *Payee* If the cheque is presented across the counter, the payee must be known as a customer of that branch or the bank giro credit must be for the credit of an account in the name of the payee.

f) *Crossings* These are an instruction to the collecting banker but if the cheque is crossed by two banks then the assumption is that the cheque has been collected for the accounts of two different persons, so the paying banker is entitled not to pay the cheque. It will be returned, marked 'crossed by two bankers' to the bank which presented it in the cheque clearing that morning.

If the cheque is crossed and presented over the counter of the paying banker for cash, then the drawer of the cheque must first 'open the crossing' by writing 'please pay cash' between the parallel lines and initialling these words or the cheque can only be credited to the account of the presenter.

g)   *Alterations* All alterations must be signed by the drawer, although initialledalterations are tolerated.

An alteration renders a cheque invalid because it is no longer the customer's instruction to the banker (unless authorized). Banks have clear difficulties, therefore, with clever alterations and undetectable changes. The courts allow banks protection provided they have taken 'reasonable care' to detect alterations.

2. The back of the cheque

Hopefully, this will be blank, meaning that the cheque has been collected for the account of the payee. Any endorsements must contain the endorsement of the payee. This is evidence that the cheque has passed through the payee's hands and that he or she intended it to be credited to the account of a third party.

Also, any mutilations will be more apparent on the back of a cheque than on the front. If the cheque is completely mutilated, then the back should bear the confirmation of the collecting banker that the mutilation was accidental and not because the drawer intended the cheque to be destroyed. Such confirmation should be signed by an authorized signatory of the collecting bank.

The back of the cheque will also carry the cheque guarantee card details (where applicable), these having been placed there by the Payee rather than the drawer (as discussed in Chapter 9).

3. Elsewhere

a)   The staff member responsible for paying the cheque must check the branch records of stopped cheques; in particular, is there a stop not yet on the computer? Except where the cheque is presented over the counter or by post or by hand as a special presentation, the computer will today detect such cheques.

b)   There must also be a check to see that there is no legal bar to payment, such as:

- death, bankruptcy or mental incapacity of the customer;

- a garnishee order, by which a third party can freeze a credit balance on an account if he or she can prove to the court that the customer owes him or her money which has been the subject of a court judgment;

- a confiscation order where the customer has been convicted of a criminal offence;

- a Mareva injunction, which can be issued by the court in cases where the ownership of a balance is in dispute and which freezes the balance for the time being.

c) Are there sufficient funds on the account? Reference to management or at least to a lending officer may be necessary before the cheque can be paid.

d) Is the signature on the cheque in accordance with the mandate given to the bank by the customer? For instance, an agent may be empowered to sign cheques. If so, is there a limit on the amount of the cheque which the agent can sign and is the cheque within this limit? If the customer is a limited company, are the signatories entitled to sign cheques?

e) Does the signature appear to be that of the customer? For this, the specimen signature given by the customer may have to be consulted for comparison. If the customer's original signature is substantially different from that on the cheque, the cheque may have to be returned marked 'signature differs' or 'signature requires drawer's confirmation'. In practice, a telephone call to the customer should resolve the matter.

Stops

A customer has the right to countermand payment of a cheque – in other words stop it – right up to the moment when the bank pays it. Today, a fee is usually levied for this service. Customers may telephone a stop, but the request must be confirmed in writing, usually using the bank's official 'stop request' form. All the details of the cheque, including the number, must be quoted accurately.

In *Westminster Bank v Hilton* (1926), the stop request form bore the wrong cheque number so the cheque was paid. The bank spotted that the cheque in their hands bore a different number to the one which they had been instructed not to pay and tried in vain to contact H. The bank then assumed that the cheque was a duplicate and paid it. Later, cheques were returned for lack of funds because the balance on the account was lower (by the amount of the paid cheque) than the customer thought. H, therefore, sued but lost. It was held that the bank had done its utmost to carry out the instruction to stop payment.

In *Curtice v London, City & Midland Bank* (1908), C sent a telegram to the bank stopping a cheque. It was delivered after business hours and, the next day, was left at the bottom of the bank's letterbox. The cheque was therefore paid and C sued. It was held that the stop had not come into the hands of the bank when the cheque was paid and, therefore, the bank was not liable for breach of contract.

In *Burnett v Westminster Bank* (1966), B had accounts at the Bromley and Borough (Southwark) branches of the bank and altered the name of the branch on a cheque – but not the computer coding at the foot. That branch, the one whose name B had written on the cheque, was told of the stop but the computer directed the cheque to the other branch. This branch, unaware of the stop, paid the cheque and B sued. He won. In spite of notices in cheque books that cheques will be applied only to the accounts for which they have been printed, the court held that a bank must notify any stops to other branches where the customer maintains accounts.

Consider the summary table below.

Statutory protection for the paying banker

Risks	Protection
A forged or unauthorised endorsement	s60 of the Bills of Exchange Act 1882, provided that the cheque is paid in good faith and in the ordinary course of business.

Collecting bank's customer has no title to the cheque	s80 of the Bills of Exchange Act 1882, provided that the cheque is paid in good faith, without negligence and in accordance with the crossing. This protection is extended to 'A/c payee' cheques by s2 of the Cheques Act 1992.
No endorsement or irregular endorsement	s1 of the Cheques Act 1957, provided the cheque is paid in good faith and in the ordinary course of business. This protection is extended to 'A/c payee' cheques by s3 of the Cheques Act 1992.

Other risks

These include:

a)   wrongly debiting a customer with cheques not intended for that account,

b)   wrongful dishonour of a cheque and

c)   payment of a cheque bearing a forged signature.

There is no statutory protection.

Wrongly debiting an account and wrongly dishonouring a cheque can lead to an action for breach of contract.

Wrongly dishonouring a cheque can lead to an action for libel from a business customer. In *Davidson v Barclays Bank* (1940), for example, the bank had paid a stopped cheque and then returned a cheque for the amount of £2.78 (£2 15s. 6d.) marked 'Not Sufficient'. The amount was a large sum then and the court held that the words constituted libel, implying that D had written a cheque when the account had insufficient funds.

Paying a cheque on a forged signature is conversion, ie allowing funds to pass into the hands of a person who is not the true owner.

There is no protection if the forged signature is that of the drawer but, as you have seen above, s60 of the Bills of Exchange Act 1882 may afford protection if the forgery is that of a necessary endorsement.

Returning cheques

Cheques are returned to the collecting banker by first-class post with the reason written on the top left-hand corner, usually in red. Below are some of the more common reasons and most are inoffensive, although we all know what 'Refer to Drawer' really means – insufficient money in the account. However, its literal meaning is 'discuss this with the person who signed the cheque'.

- Refer to Drawer
- Refer to Drawer, Please Represent
- Refer to Drawer, Trustee in bankruptcy appointed
- Drawer's signature required
- Another signature required
- No account
- Out of date
- Post-dated
- Signature requires drawer's confirmation
- Signature differs
- Orders not to pay (with or without 'awaiting confirmation')
- Drawer deceased
- Mutilated cheque

All banks keep registers of inward and outward returned cheques and now charge their customers for the expense involved.

Cleared and uncleared funds

The meaning of these terms is not always understood by customers so may have to be explained to people who wish to draw cheques against other cheques that have just been paid in or against credits that have just been received.

The terms do not refer to whether the cheques will be dishonoured but to whether or not the collecting banker has received payment for them at the clearing house. Thus, CHAPS and BACS items represent cleared funds to a bank because its account at the Bank of England is credited the same day.

Items remitted in the cheque clearing do not become 'cleared funds' until the third working day after they were collected – the day the entries appear in the bank's accounts at the Bank of England. Moreover, they might be returned as 'unpaids' until noon the following day. So, banks are reluctant to pay cheques drawn by customers who rely on these uncleared cheques – 'uncleared effects' as they are called – to provide the funds.

Items in the credit clearings are cleared funds when received at the beneficiary's branch. However, if they comprise cheques drawn on other banks or branches, then there is the possibility of such cheques being dishonoured and returned and debited to the payee's account a day or two after the credit was received.

Surprisingly to many customers, although banker's drafts and building society cheques will not be dishonoured, they still take three days to become cleared funds. As soon as funds become cleared, the bank will allow interest to be credited on them, if applicable, and will be able to use these funds to pay any cheques drawn by the customer.

Summary

- It is vital to distinguish between the collecting bank, which acts usually for the payee of a cheque, and the paying bank, which acts for the drawer. Both banks have to examine cheques very carefully.

- The collecting bank examines a cheque for: date; words and figures in agreement; whether an endorsement is needed; whether the crossing bears the words 'not negotiable' or 'A/c payee only'; whether alterations have been initialled; the presence of a signature; and any sign of mutilation.

- Collecting banks obtain statutory protection for collecting cheques for people who are not the true owners, provided that they collect for: a customer; in good faith; and without negligence.

- The paying bank scrutinizes a cheque for: date; words and figures in agreement; whether the cheque is crossed to another bank or organization other than the collecting bank or payee; whether the signature is genuine and in accordance with the mandate; whether there is a stop on the cheque and whether there are sufficient funds on the account.

- Paying banks get statutory protection under two headings:

  a) For an endorsement that is forged, irregular or missing, if they pay the cheque in good faith and in the ordinary course of business.

  b) If the collecting bank's customer had no title to the cheque, then the paying bank is protected if the cheque is paid in good faith, without negligence and in accordance with the crossing.

- There is no protection for paying banks who pay forged cheques, or who libel their customers by dishonouring cheques when there were sufficient funds on the account.

Cleared funds are those for which the bank has received payment by having its account at the Bank of England credited.

Further Reading – Chapter 11

Arora A, (1993) *Cases and Materials in Banking Law*, Pitman (Chapters 6 to 8).

Richardson D, (1983) *A Guide to Negotiable Instruments,* Butterworths.

12 Elementary lending

Objectives

After studying this chapter you should be able to:

☐   **State the elements of good lending.**

☐   **Describe how lending principles can be applied to different cases.**

☐   **Explain the role of credit scoring in modern lending.**

Introduction

Whole careers have been spent in lending and in taking security for loans and overdrafts, so what can be included in a single chapter can only be very rudimentary. But lending is the banking skill and banks can fail if their loans are bad. Moreover, banks can lose profits if they do not seize opportunities for good lending, so the subject is very important. However, lending skills come with practice and experience rather than from reading a book.

We shall approach the subject by looking at the lending acronym CAMPARI and ICE, which recalls important principles of lending; then we describe the modern technique of credit scoring.

Principles of Lending

The principles or 'canons' of lending apply to large corporations as well as to small personal borrowers. Credit scoring criteria (which we shall look at later) draw heavily on these factors too.

Common acronyms that recall these canons and act as an aid to memory include:

- 3C's   (Character, Capability, Capital)

- IPARTS   (Integrity, Purpose, Amount, Repayment, Terms and Security)

- 4 C's   (adds Connection to the 3 C's)

- CAMPARI   (Character, Ability, Means, Purpose, Amount, Repayment, Insurance)

- CAMPARI and ICE   (adds Interest, Charges and Extras)

- PARSERS   (Person, Amount, Repayment, Security, Expediency, Remuneration, Services)

- CRIS   (Character, Repayment, Incentive, Security)

It should be noted that in each of the acronyms the criteria concerning the personality or character of the borrower rank highly whereas identification of the security on offer is only considered after repayment has been reviewed. This is very much as it should be. Bad lending propositions do not get better just because security is available they should be judged on their merits and then security sought to provide for unforeseen circumstances which may prevent repayment coming from the primary source.

The following sections discuss the popular acronym – CAMPARI and ICE:

Character

The borrower, who seeks to be lent money entrusted to the bank by its depositors, must be of the utmost integrity – somebody who will keep his or her word and who can be believed.

Much relies on a borrower's track record with the bank or, in the case of new borrowers, on the manager's skill and experience in interviews with borrowers or on the borrower's credit history obtained from a credit reference agency.

Ability

This is vital for business, whether or not loans are involved. The borrower must be, at the very least, proficient, if not an expert at his or her job or in his or her profession. Is there any hint of incompetence? If the customer has been with the bank for many years, there should be some clues in the file but, if the request is from somebody unknown to the bank, searching but tactful questions must be asked at the interview.

Means/Margin

How much of his or her own money is the borrower using and how much of other people's, including the bank's? These figures will be apparent from the request from the customer and it is important to remember that many borrowers under-estimate the amount that they need to borrow.

A good rule of thumb would be that a bank would not wish to put in more money than the borrower. The bank takes an equal risk on the success of the venture (unless secured) but receives interest only on borrowings rather than a share of profits.

How much money is being put into the project by the borrower and how much by the banks and other lenders? The latter could include an HP company or finance house while business customers often finance themselves partly by delaying payment for goods and services bought from their suppliers.

Purpose

The purpose of the borrowing is extremely important. When personal loans were launched in 1958, a loan for a holiday would have been rejected because the loan's purpose was unacceptable. Today 12-month loans for a holiday are often agreed by banks.

However there is a more important reason why purpose is important. This concerns commercial lending. The purpose for which the loan is used will affect the finances of the borrowing firm, and the cash-flow projections for the next two or three years will vary according to the use to which the money is put. For instance, if a firm buys the freehold of its existing shop we can expect to see no rent payments in the cash-flow projections – not a dramatic change – but if, instead, the money is used to buy stock then we should see cash soon coming into the business from the sales of that stock (assuming that sales are for cash and not credit).

In addition the bank would wish to ensure that it was not lending for an illegal or nefarious purpose!

Amount

Again, the borrower may ask for less than is needed, in the hope of making the request seem more attractive to the lender or because the cash-flow forecasts are wrong. Many honest borrowers underestimate their cash needs. Even where a property is to be purchased have the legal and professional fees been considered? Have the running costs incurred before income can be generated been covered?

Repayment and term

How is the loan to be repaid? There are two main sources:

- from income, eg the sales of a firm's output or the wages/salary of a personal borrower;

- from the sales of an existing asset, eg an existing house, as with a bridging loan; an insurance policy maturing, as with a loan for a world cruise for a customer in his or her late 50s or early 60s; or the sale of the old premises when a firm moves to a new site.

Whatever the repayment source, it must be known before the loan is granted and be agreeable to both lender and borrower. Repayment must not stretch the borrower too far. Has the personal borrower shown an ability to save the amount of the monthly repayment in the recent past? Does the business borrower's cash-flow forecast cater adequately for regular repayments and interest?

This part of the acronym also looks at the period of borrowing. Personal loans can go to five years and home loans are – in theory

– for 25 years. However, many people sell their house long before the 25 years are up and take out a new mortgage for the new house. In fact, the average life of a mortgage is only about eight years.

The term of the borrowing is related to the purpose of the borrowing. Funds borrowed by a company to buy stock should be repaid when the sale proceeds of the stock are received – usually within months – although fresh borrowing will then occur to finance more purchases of stock. An overdraft is the appropriate form of bank finance here. However, a loan to buy the freehold site of a factory could be repaid over eight or ten years.

For personal lending, a loan for an annual holiday ought to be repaid before the next holiday, but a loan for, say, double glazing or a new kitchen could be repaid over seven years. Loans for plant, machinery or cars should take into consideration the useful life of the asset purchased.

Insurance (Security)

This point is deliberately put last because the decision whether or not to lend should have been made on the other six points. Obviously, lending covered by security must be more attractive than unsecured lending but the availability of security may influence the lender to agree to a doubtful proposition. The questions that must be asked are:

- Is security offered?

- If not, can some acceptable security be found?

- Is the security offered adequate?

- If not, can more be found?

- What is the nature of the security? (see next chapter)

- Who will deposit the security?

- When will the security be deposited?

Again, as a general rule a banker should not extend a loan until the security documentation is complete or, at least, until the security has been deposited.

Additional insurance, in the strictest meaning of the word, also needs to be considered under this heading. For companies, insuring the lives of key directors will be a comfort to the bank. For personal borrowers insurance to cover sickness, unemployment or death will also be sought.

...and ICE

This brings us to the income for the bank to be gained from agreeing to the proposition:

Interest
Is the margin over LIBOR or base rate sufficient to compensate for any risk involved for the bank? Typically, risky industries (eg: construction) will be quoted a higher margin over base than lower risk ones (eg: agriculture). Similarly larger firms would exact finer rates than sole proprietors. Favourable interest rates are one of the reasons for the increasing trend for very large firms to bypass the banks entirely and borrow directly from the markets (disintermediation).

Commission
In addition to annual interest, borrowers may be faced with commission, sometimes termed as 'arrangement fee' to be paid when the loan is drawn down. Very occasionally it is added to the principal amount borrowed. The difference between Commission (Charges) and Interest is that interest compensates the bank for the risk undertaken while Commission compensates for the work involved in granting and monitoring the loan or overdraft facility.

Extras
Are there other products – eg insurance, travel facilities, unit trusts, private banking – that might be offered to the customer? Are there other members of the family or other businesses in the group to which products can be sold? Cross-selling is becoming more and more important as more banks compete for the same customers. To a certain extent customers can be 'locked in' by purchasing services

from their bank, and in addition banks are more able to target services to groups of existing customers as they have considerable information about their spending habits already.

The weakness of using an acronym is that it is backward-looking. For business borrowing the lending officer also needs to go through forecasts of the accounts, including cash-flow, for several years ahead to see if the borrowing can be serviced, ie repayments made of part of the principal sum as well as payment of interest. For personal borrowers this also means judging the stability of a person's employment and his or her capacity to earn at the level needed to service the loan. Professionals such as solicitors or doctors can show an ability to earn high salaries easily but a production worker in an area of high unemployment may not, especially if fleeting overtime payments are needed to make the repayments.

In addition CAMPARI and ICE does not consider a very commercial feature of lending that other acronyms (such as PARSERS and 4C's) do. This is the relationship between the borrower and other customers. PARSERS includes Expediency as a feature and 4C's looks at Connections. Clearly a bank will not wish to sour its relationship with a good connected account by refusing a loan to, say, the Managing Director's son or daughter.

Illustrative Case studies

CASE 1: Bill Adams – Bridging Loan
Bill Adams, Regional Sales Manager for a large grocery wholesaler, wishes to move house to both upgrade his accommodation and to be closer to the head office of his employer. Because the move is voluntary the employer cannot assist the move and Bill must finance it himself.

Bill's present house is for sale at a price of £100,000 and is subject to a Building Society mortgage of £50,000. The new house will cost £150,000 and a mortgage of £100,000 has already been agreed by the same society but is available only when the present mortgage loan is repaid.

There is no firm buyer for the present property yet but Bill is being pressed to exchange contracts and commit himself to the purchase of the new one.

The bank is asked to lend the full purchase price of the new property, to be repaid from the proceeds of the new mortgage (£100,000) and the equity in the old property (£50,000).

Considerations for the bank:

- Is Bill a trustworthy customer with a good track record?

- Are the properties valued correctly?

- Can Bill pay the estimated monthly interest?

- What will happen if the present property has to drop in price to achieve a sale?

- Have allowances been made for Legal and Estate Agent costs?

- Are any other mortgages outstanding?

- Can the bridgeover requirement be reduced in any way? – eg: family help/mortgage from a different provider.

Bank decision:
On the face of it the bank will have to decline – at least until Bill has exchanged contracts on his present property. Even then the bank must be sure that the interest can be paid by Bill in addition to the other expenses he will incur (carpets, curtains etc).

CASE 2: Cliff Ramsbotham – Overdraft
Cliff Ramsbotham and his family have farmed the same area of the Derbyshire Peak District for generations. They own their own farmhouse, valued at £80,000, and rent 300 acres of hillside grazing land from the Peak National Park Authority. Cliff's main asset is a herd of 500 sheep (200 breeding ewes and 300 followers valued at £40,000 and £33,000 respectively). Lambs born in the springtime are fattened and sold at either November or May sales. By May the cycle has begun again. Farm income is supplemented by renting two farm cottages to tourists during the summer and an adult son has a part-time job as a Park Ranger and Mountain Rescue team member.

Accounts for the past three years show the farm in a steady state with enough income being generated to allow the family to live comfortably. Income and expenditure from last year was as follows:

Income

Sale of lambs	£37,000	
Rent of cottages	£4,000	
Grants	£8,000	
Other income	£3,000	
		£52,000

Expenditure

Rent of hillside land	£15,000	
Livestock feed	£8,500	
Drawings	£20,000	
Veterinary Services	£2,500	
Other (fuel etc)	£1,500	
		£47,500

Surplus / deficit		**£4,500**

Cliff maintains an exemplary account with the bank and has always honoured agreements made. The present overdraft limit is set at £10,000 but this is only used in the two months before the bi-annual livestock sales which Cliff attends.

Cliff now wishes to increase the size of his herd both to utilize his rented acreage fully and to provide a better income for his son. He asks to borrow £12,000 by extension of the overdraft in order to buy a further 60 breeding ewes. The overdraft would be reduced to the original £10,000 over the next year using sale proceeds from the progeny of the new livestock (estimated at £12,000).

Considerations for the bank:

- Normal canons of lending apply even though this is a specialist area.

- Cliff is an experienced farmer, runs a moderately successful farm and has always honoured agreements in the past.

- Cliff's contribution to the venture is difficult to see. He wishes to borrow the whole of the purchase price but will find the costs of feedstock and veterinary services from his own resources.

- At first sight the repayment over one year appears ambitious and leaves no leeway should lamb prices fall. As it is, the expectation of price rises to £120 per lamb may be unrealistic.

- Purpose is appropriate for bank finance with seasonal sales as a repayment mechanism.

- Surplus income appears to be fairly marginal at £4,500 pa. It is used to replace around 20 older ewes each year but should be enough to pay interest and charges too.

- Farming is traditionally very low-risk and so a lower interest rate would be indicated.

- Security may be available in the form of a mortgage over the farmhouse.

- Cross-selling opportunities for leasing of agricultural equipment, insurance and pensions are apparent.

Bank decision:
The bank would probably agree to this overdraft, given Cliff's past record and experience but would require some form of security to cover the additional borrowing. Cliff may be reticent to mortgage the family home but may be able to offer other security in the form of a Life Policy, Shares or an Agricultural Charge (floating charge over farming assets).

The bank would monitor the overdraft carefully to ensure that the expected sale proceeds were received. In addition the bank may be prepared to allow full repayment of the additional overdraft over two years in order to allow Cliff some breathing space.

These case studies show that the lending decision is rarely straightforward, rarely simple and that no two cases are ever the same. The strength in the lending acronyms is that they cover all types of case if they are interpreted widely enough.

Credit scoring

This is a practice used to help lending decisions for personal borrowers. Credit Scoring is routinely performed as soon as an account is opened, aiding the decision whether to issue a cheque guarantee card or debit card immediately. Banks update and augment the customer's score by analysing account behaviour once the account is running.

In basic Credit Scoring various characteristics of the potential borrower and the loan request are each given a rating or score. The numbers are then added up and read off against a range of risk probabilities. This range is calculated from past experience of the lender (sometimes of other lenders).

Thus, a bank or building society may take a policy decision to reject all personal loan applications where there is more than a 2% chance of the loan not being repaid. The potential borrower's score will then be read across to this risk percentage, showing whether the risk is within the 2% acceptability level.

One benefit of Credit Scoring is that it is consistent and that its success (or otherwise) can be measured. In addition the pass mark can be altered up or down as the lending or marketing policy of the bank changes. Direct or Internet banks use Credit Scoring extensively because they are unable to meet face to face with customers.

The scoring process indicates the level of risk associated with the proposition, not whether that particular loan will be a bad debt. Moreover, the scoring can always be overridden by a manager who takes other factors into consideration. The credit score factors may include:

- sex, age;
- place of residence and length of time there;
- if recently moved to that address, the previous address and length of time there;
- whether or not on the telephone;
- whether owner-occupier, tenant, living with parents or in a hostel;
- occupation and employer;

- salary and other income;

- monthly outgoings;

- bankers and (if applicable) building society;

- other creditors – including credit and store cards.

Although Credit Scoring criteria are designed to measure risk statistically they can be interpreted using the CAMPARI framework. An example may be the presence of a telephone – indicating the ability to pay a regular bill. Of course the common use of mobile phones may decrease the value of this measure.

Scoring is often done by computer, with the results shown on the screen immediately. Applications will also be vetted via a Credit Bureau to reveal any county court judgments or bankruptcy orders. Overriding is possible, particularly if the potential borrower is part of an important business or family connection for the branch. For instance, it would be foolish to refuse a loan to an employee of a large company banking with the branch or to the daughter of a very wealthy family, solely on the arithmetic of a computer.

Summary

- Lending principles can be learnt from various phrases and words that act as summaries.

- Reviewing the character of the borrower and the proposition are considered before the security being offered.

- Lending acronyms are applicable to both business and personal borrowers.

- Credit scoring is now computer-based, enabling borrowing requests to be assessed against what head office deems to be an acceptable level of risk.

- Credit scoring does not predict whether a proposed loan will be good or bad and the result of the computer assessment can be overridden by a senior official.

Further Reading – Chapter 12

Rouse C N, (2002), *Banker's Lending Techniques,* Financial World Publishing.

Rouse C N, (1992), *Applied Lending Techniques*, CIB Books.

Anderton B (Ed), (1995), *Current Issues in Financial Services*, Macmillan, Chapter 8.

13 Elementary security for lending

Objectives

After studying this chapter you should be able to:

- [ ] Discuss the importance of security.

- [ ] List and apply the steps needed to take security.

- [ ] List and explain some of the major factors involved in taking security.

- [ ] Describe some of the major forms of banking security.

Security

In the last chapter we looked at the questions that should be asked by a lender before considering security. Security protects the lender in case things go wrong. The assets commonly charged as security are mainly: land (including buildings), stocks and shares, and life assurance policies. In law these are all 'choses in action', assets evidenced by documents (certificates, deeds etc). Banks much prefer dealing with securities where ownership can be evidenced in this way rather than with chattels such as cars, plant and machinery or furniture. However valuable this may be, it cannot be charged or controlled as effectively as land, shares or life policies.

This chapter can cover only the key themes in a basic way but it is important to recognize that security-taking is based on contract law and that a failure to observe the normal rules of contract can render security contracts void, leaving the bank with an unsecured loan. It is also important to see that bank security-taking procedures are designed to ensure that the security cannot be challenged and that it is protected from problems that may occur while it is being held.

When is a contract not a contract?

In the same way that banks must ensure that accounts should be opened only for customers with legal capacity who fully intend to create a legal relationship with the bank, so security contracts must ensure that the depositor cannot later avoid the contract due to some legal defect. This is particularly important since bank charge forms are complex and lengthy documents and often a third party (not the borrower) deposits the security to secure the account of the borrower. Legal cases have forced banks to advise security providers to use independent solicitors to assist in the execution of security documents.

Key problems that banks need to be aware of are: Mistake, Misrepresentation and Undue Influence.

Mistake
A serious mistake of fact about a contract will affect the contract's validity to the extent that the contract will be void. This may be mutual mistake as to subject matter but in banking cases the mistake is normally fundamental, fraudulently induced and made without negligence on the part of the person claiming to avoid the contract. An ancient defence of *Non est factum* or 'It is not my deed' can be used in these circumstances.

In the case of *Carlisle & Cumberland Bank v Bragg* (1911) the borrower took the guarantee form to the guarantor for signature. Here the nature of the document was mistaken as an insurance document and the guarantor held not to be liable. Although a guarantee is, strictly, not a tangible security the case illustrates this aspect of the law well. In *Saunders v Anglia Building Society* (1970) this was overruled because Mrs Saunders had signed without reading the document (her glasses were broken). Claims of mistake can only be made where the claimant has not been negligent themselves – see also *Lloyds Bank v Waterhouse* (1991).

Misrepresentation

Misrepresentation renders a contract voidable at the option of the party misled. For misrepresentation to operate there must be a false statement of specific, verifiable fact and not law. In this way an opinion or even silence cannot be construed as misrepresentation.

The party misled will have relied on the false statement which will have had a significant, rather than trivial, impact on their decision to execute the security. In the case of *Mackenzie v Royal Bank of Canada* (1934) Mrs Mackenzie was able to avoid a guarantee given in favour of her husband's business because the bank wrongly misrepresented to her that her shares, deposited earlier, would be returned to her. In the case of *Lloyds Bank v Waterhouse* (1991) the bank misrepresented the nature of a guarantee to the father of their borrower. The father, being illiterate, asked questions about the document but was not liable under the guarantee as the bank's answers were inadequate.

Duress and Undue Influence

In the more recent case of Kingsnorth Trust Ltd. v Bell (1986) a husband misled his wife as to the purpose of the advance made and so the charge over the matrimonial home she created was voidable for undue influence. Duress and undue influence renders a contract voidable at the option of the party influenced. Undue influence is assumed by the law in a number of relationships:

- Parent – Child;
- Priest – Disciple;
- Doctor – Patient;
- Trustee – Beneficiary;

- Solicitor – Client; and

- Guardian – Infant.

In other relationships undue influence must be proved. In this way Mr Bundy, in *Lloyds Bank Ltd v Bundy* (1974) was able to avoid the guarantee given to support his son due to the fact that the bank manager came to his house to obtain his signature and that the bank was looked on as a financial advisor.

Recent years have seen a number of cases involving undue influence although *National Westminster Bank plc v Morgan* (1985) remains the most influential. In this case the court would only allow the contract to be avoided where the party influenced had suffered material disadvantage as a result of executing the guarantee or charge.

Avoiding the pitfalls

The case of *O'Brien v Barclays Bank plc* (1993) laid down rules for banks when taking security. In all cases Independent Legal Advice should be offered and a note made if it is offered and not taken up. Independent Legal Advice is where the charge form is sent to the depositor's solicitor (not the bank's) for the document to be explained, witnessed and attested by the solicitor.

Bank Charge forms – key clauses

Bank charge forms are, necessarily long and comprehensive statements of the agreement between the security provider and the bank. In most cases the bank provides the pre-printed charge form to the provider advising that Independent Legal Advice should be sought before it is signed.

Solicitors who are asked to explain bank charge forms will need to explain some key clauses:

The Whole Debt Clause
Known as the 'whole debt' or 'all monies' clause this ensures that any monies or liabilities owing by the debtor at any time and on any

account or under any guarantee are secured. A separate agreement is needed if the security is to relate only to one loan and not to other indebtedness.

> *"...all and every the sum and sums of money which now are or shall at any time be owing to the Bank by me anywhere on my current account or any other account..."*

EXTRACT FROM ABC BANK PLC DIRECT DEPOSIT OF STOCKS & SHARES.

Continuing security

By being expressed as a continuing security the security does not become invalid when the borrowing is repaid (as on a fluctuating current account). The rule in Clayton's case is, therefore, avoided.

Consideration

This clause speaks of the value passing from the Bank to the chargor

> *"In consideration of XYZ Bank plc (the Bank) giving time credit banking facilities or other accommodation to:*
>
> *NAME AND ADDRESS OF DEBTOR*
> *NOW*
> *NAME AND ADDRESS OF GUARANTOR*
>
> *hereby guarantees payment to the Bank on demand of..."*

EXTRACT FROM XYZ BANK PLC GUARANTEE.

Joint and several liability

As with J&S liability on account balances security can be deposited Jointly and Severally. This means that if one party fails to fulfil his part of the contract (eg; he dies) the other party(ies) is/are wholly liable. This clause is particularly useful in guarantees.

Demand

Various clauses cover the situation where the Bank makes demand under its security:

Personal covenant to repay
This marks the point where the Statute of Limitations starts to run – six years for a simple contract eg: Memorandum of Deposit of Shares, twelve years for a contract under seal eg: Mortgage of Land.

Service of Demand
This states that demand will be sent to the last known address of the debtor or guarantor. Demand will be effective, therefore, even if the debtor no longer lives there.

Conclusive Evidence
To avoid doubt regarding the amount of the demand this clause states that a certificate given by an officer of the Bank will be conclusive evidence of any legal proceedings against the debtor.

Testing for good security
The banker must also know when a particular security that is offered will make a good security for an advance. As with lending a number of acronyms have been developed to help remember the key features. One such acronym is **MAST**. The letters stand for:

Marketability — the asset should be able to be sold easily;

Ascertainability of Value — it should be easy to obtain a value for the asset;

Simplicity of Title — it should be easy to ascertain the legal owner of the security and, thus, the person(s) who must execute the mortgage or charge.

Transferability of Title — it must be easy to transfer title to the bank so that the asset can be sold if required.

Another phrase to remember is **Very Little Money Indeed** and the letters stand for:

Value   — it should be easy to obtain a value
                                   for the asset;

Legal mortgage   — it should be possible to take a legal
                                   mortgage;

Marketability   — the asset should be able to be sold
                                   easily;

Increase in value   — the value of the asset should rise
                                   during the period of the loan.

Land is a common security but particular types of land will not pass
the MAST or VLMI tests. For example: a charge over a domestic
residence, in a Registered Land area and in a popular housing area
where values are stable or increasing passes the test and makes a
good security. A derelict factory with contaminated land in an area
of high unemployment and numerous other factory sites will not
pass the test.

Care must be taken when applying these tests but with common
sense, experience and access to professional valuers and surveyors
the job is made easier.

Valuation

All assets to which the lender looks for security should be capable
of being accurately valued and these values should be checked
regularly during the period of the borrowing.

Let us see how values can be obtained for the major items of
security.

Land

Land and buildings are usually very acceptable as security for
lenders but a windmill or former lighthouse may be difficult to
value if offered as security by the owner.

Banks invariably seek professional valuations of all property,
domestic and commercial, especially since the property slump of

the late 1980s and the years of negative equity. The trends in the market and long-term stability of value are as important as the selling price today. A useful rule-of-thumb for buildings is 'What price did a similar one fetch when sold recently?' but in the case of a windmill or lighthouse there may be no recent local examples to serve as a guide!

Commercial properties invariably need a professional valuation by a surveyor, as do many more unusual private houses. Banks instruct valuers to provide valuations on various bases:

Gone Concern – or Forced Sale Value. – This is the worst price that the property would achieve if auctioned. It has the advantage of being the 'worst case scenario' for the bank and should guide lending decisions. If a property is sold at auction the bank will obtain its repayment more quickly than if the property sold for a higher sum after months of negotiation with prospective buyers.

Going Concern – This is the valuation (usually for business premises) that indicates the price that would be paid by a buyer wishing to continue the business uninterrupted. It is useful to show the true value of a business. It represents the 'best case scenario' and will, therefore, be viewed carefully by a banker.

Stocks and shares

Lenders prefer these to be in public limited companies (Plcs) quoted on the Stock Exchange, because daily prices are available in the *Stock Exchange Daily List* or the *Financial Times.* A lender will also prefer a mix of companies, rather than shares of only one company. The shares of most such companies can be sold quite easily, although for the very smallest the seller may have to drop the price to find a ready buyer.

If the shares are not quoted on the Stock Exchange, an independent accountant may be called up to provide a valuation derived from the latest audited balance sheet.

Life assurance policies

These are the easiest asset to value because the company that has issued them will provide, promptly, a surrender value, ie the amount which it will pay when the assured surrenders his or her rights under the policy. They may also be sold in a small market for second-hand policies. Sale of life policies will often be more beneficial than surrender but premiums must have been paid up to date.

Legal mortgage

Mortgages are processes by which other people obtain a right to use our assets if we do not repay them the money which we have borrowed from them. In this section, we confine the discussion to mortgages given by the borrowers – not by other people (eg relations).

Mortgages are of two types – legal and equitable – deriving their names from the two types of law – common law and equity – which developed and were administered separately until 1875. Lenders prefer legal mortgages because they can proceed to sell the asset should the need arise. Legal mortgages give the lender (the mortgagee) immediate rights to sell the asset if the mortgagor defaults on the debt, without involving the mortgagor any further.

Equitable mortgages give the lender certain rights against the borrower and, if lenders wish to sell the asset mortgaged to them, they will have to get the co-operation of the borrower. If needs be, the lenders may have to seek a court order for the sale. Each bank will have its own standard form of equitable mortgage, in which the borrower (the mortgagor) undertakes to sign a legal mortgage should he or she fail to repay the debt.

Although the equitable mortgage is weaker than the legal mortgage when remedies are viewed it does have the advantage of being able to be created more quickly – simply by deposit of the security with the intention that it be treated as collateral. A legal mortgage requires that a mortgage form be executed and notification given to the appropriate registry of ownership (except for shares) for it to be valid.

A further protection for the legal mortgage comes when the date of creation of the mortgage is reviewed. A legal mortgage created before an equitable mortgage or another legal mortgage will always have priority. This is the case even where there is a pre-existing equitable mortgage that the mortgagee had no notice of. For an equitable mortgage to have priority over a legal mortgage the equitable mortgage must be created first in time and notice of it must be given so that subsequent mortgagees are aware of it (See Fig 15).

Figure 15
Legal (L) and Equitable (E) mortgages

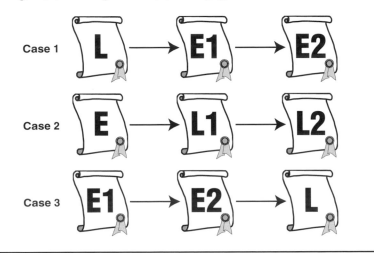

Notes:

Case 1:   The Legal Mortgage 'L' has priority followed by 'E1' and then 'E2'.

Case 2:   'L1' only has priority over 'L2'. It could have priority over 'E' if the mortgagee (bank) had no notice of 'E' prior to the creation of 'L1'.

Case 3:   'L' only has priority over 'E1' and /or 'E2' if it had no notice of these earlier charges.

Land

Most people think that mortgages must be over land because they are so common – we all give a mortgage over our house when we borrow most of the purchase price of it. Legal mortgages are far more common than equitable mortgages, with both types of mortgagees holding the deeds which evidence the borrower's ownership. Most banks will retain the deeds at the branch where the loan is kept but some building societies prefer a central store to hold all their deeds.

Once the borrower has parted with his or her deeds to the lender, the borrower cannot sell the property without the lender's consent. Thus, the security is pretty safe.

Stocks and shares

Stocks and shares can be charged under a legal mortgage but, when the borrowers want to sell them, the lenders must give their agreement. This can be quite restrictive, particular in a fast-moving market, so lenders are usually content to take an equitable mortgage, releasing the shares when the owner wishes to sell, in exchange for the cash proceeds or another block of shares into which the owner has switched. The bank's standard form of equitable mortgage will contain an undertaking from the mortgagor to execute a legal mortgage when required.

If the shares are unquoted, then the bank may require a legal mortgage unless this causes embarrassment to the customer, eg the company may belong to a close-knit family.

Life assurance policies

Strictly, these are not mortgaged but are assigned under a procedure laid down by Act of Parliament. The lender must give notice to the assurance company.

Marketability

If the lender has got title to the property/asset as a result of the borrower's default, the asset is sold, the debt is repaid out of the proceeds, plus the expenses of the sale, and any balance is handed back to the borrower. Thus, a speedy sale would be ideal but, as we all know from the recent past, house prices and demand for houses can go down as well as up.

Land

Land is generally sold by negotiation (private treaty) and only rarely by auction. As a rough and ready rule, a period of six months between 'putting a house on the market' and completing the sale is very good. In times of low demand, much longer periods have elapsed, and sellers have had to lower their prices drastically to achieve a sale.

Historically, however, land is marketable. Today environmental issues and the costs of cleaning up contaminated land can affect marketability and value. Land used for one purpose (industry, farming) cannot always be sold for another purpose (housing). Planning permission for a change of use or for development of land can increase marketability and value dramatically.

Stocks and shares

If these are quoted on the London Stock Exchange they are marketable, although some are more marketable than others.

Smaller companies may have a much thinner market and buy and sell prices may be wider to attract market participants.

Generally, the larger the company (such as those 'blue chip' companies making up the Financial Times 100 Share Index ('Footsie 100')), the easier it is to trade in the shares.

With private companies, the articles of association may require all sales of shares to be referred to the board of directors first. This may limit their marketability

Life assurance polices

These are easy to market because the company that issued them will send a cheque for the surrender value within a few days. In the second-hand market, the policies can be auctioned to the highest bidder or sold directly to a specialist firm which will on-sell them later to investors in such policies.

Increase in value

Ideally, security should rise steadily in value. But only life assurance policies have this quality guaranteed, provided the premiums are paid on time.

Land

In the long term, property values rise. An example can be taken from the East Midlands where a three-bedroomed detached house was bought new in 1975 for £18,000, sold in 1986 for £42,000, and put on the market for £95,000 in 1989. The house price slump at the time meant that the house sold for £85,000 eventually but by 2001 had risen in value to around £150,000. House prices rose, on average, 11-12% in 2001 and are forecast to rise more slowly (3-4%) in 2002 by a major mortgage lender.

Some property – especially shops and offices – have leasehold title, with the owner being granted a lease – a right of exclusive occupation – of (say) 99 years, at the end of which period the ownership goes back to the freeholder who granted the lease. As this date approaches, the value of the building, or more correctly the leaseholder's right to it, falls steadily because the freeholder has the right to reoccupy the property and could knock it down and redevelop the site.

Hence, a short lease does not appreciate in value – in fact, it falls. It could be charged as security for a short-term loan but certainly not for any period longer than about five years.

In brief, most property has risen in value, but can experience sharp falls in the short term.

Stocks and shares

These rise and fall in value. They must be watched almost daily by private investors. Banks, however, do not have the time to do this. Instead, they look to having a margin or surplus over the amount of the loan to cushion them against the daily rises and falls of prices. Higher-risk shares (such as South African Gold Mines) will need a higher margin but even 'solid' UK shares such as bank shares or large retailers show wide fluctuations during a year.

However, an across-the-board fall, such as that of 19 October 1987, can cause problems for both lenders and borrowers relying on these shares as security. And the fall may be gradual, in what is called a 'bear market'.

Nevertheless, since 1945 equity prices have risen faster than the rate of inflation.

Life assurance policies

As we stated earlier, the surrender values of life assurance policies usually increase steadily in value, provided the premiums are paid.

Guarantees

A guarantee is a legal undertaking by one person – the guarantor – to a lender to be responsible for the debt of another. 'If X does not pay you, I will'.

Guarantees are solemn undertakings which most guarantors do not really understand. As we saw in Chapter 7 Mr Bundy needed the Court of Appeal to rescue him from his guarantee to Lloyds Bank. Guarantees are not strictly security because the lender has to assess the credit-worthiness of the guarantor and will usually require the guarantor to charge security in support of his or her guarantee.

In 1994, a decision of the House of Lords caused more problems for lenders relying on guarantees and security charged by people (friends and relatives) other than the borrower (termed third-party security). In *Barclays Bank v O'Brien*, their Lordships held that a married woman (or partner with whom the borrower was living) must be regarded as a special type of guarantor, requiring protection from the law because of her emotional involvement with the borrower. Once the security is charged by a 'co-habitee', the lender is, to use legal jargon, placed on 'constructive notice' that there may be deceit or undue influence. The lender does not have to have actual notice.

The way for the lender to 'perfect the security/guarantee' is for the guarantrix (jargon again!) to have the form fully explained to her by an independent solicitor.

The case is very important because it introduced the principle of 'constructive notice' into the taking of guarantees and third-party security.

Nevertheless, a guarantee is better than no security at all, even though making demand upon the guarantor can result in much ill-will if not downright hostility.

Security-taking procedures

Security in the form of Land, Stocks and Shares or Life Policies must be taken correctly in order that it can be used where a borrower fails to make repayment of the advance. A simple acronym – DIVAN can help to remember the necessary steps in the security taking process:

DIVAN

Step	*Typical considerations*
D – Deposit	• Are these the original Deeds/Certificates or duplicates?
	• Has a receipt been given?
	• Are the Deeds/Certificates complete (ie: are previous mortgages, now repaid, attached?)
I – Inspect	• Who owns the security?
	• How many shares?
	• Prior charges?
	• What searches need to be made?
	• Do the providers have the power to create a mortgage?
V – Value	• How much is the security worth?
	• How often does an updated valuation need to be made?
A – Authorize	• Who must execute the security
	• Is a company seal needed?
	• How many signatures are needed?
	• Has Independent Legal Advice been offered?
N – Notify	• Where should the charge be registered to protect it?
	• What searches are needed in six months to ensure that the bank's charge is registered?

Summary

- Security should be the last factor in any credit assessment, being designed to act as a 'long stop' to protect the lender if the lending does not go to plan.

- Security must be taken correctly because it can be avoided later as a contract by claims of Mistake, Misrepresentation or Duress and Undue Influence

- Bank charge forms contain key clauses which must be understood. These include the Whole Debt clause and the Continuing Security clause.

- The qualities that make an asset good security can be remembered by the phrase Very Little Money Indeed:

  - Valuation is easy

  - Legal mortgage is possible

  - Marketability is good

  - Increases in value are probable

  or

  MAST

  - Marketability

  - Ascertainability of Value

  - Simplicity of Title

  - Transferability of Title

- Legal mortgages are preferred by lenders because they confer rights against the asset mortgaged without having to contact the borrower (mortgagor).

- Equitable mortgages confer rights against the person mortgaging the asset. This person – the mortgagor – must be involved in disposing of the asset.

- Land is a good form of security because it usually possesses all four characteristics – except in times of falling house prices! Stocks & shares and Life Policies are also useful security.

- Guarantees are, in effect, potential repayments from third parties and guarantors need to be assessed for their creditworthiness.

- The DIVAN procedure for taking security helps banks to ensure that the charge is legally watertight.

Further Reading – Chapter 13

Amin V, (1994), *Bankers' Securities – A Practical and Legal Guide,* CIB Books.

Roberts G, (1999), *Law Relating to Financial Services.* CIB Publishing, Chapter 6.

14 Bankers and insolvency

Objectives

After studying this chapter you should be able to:

- [ ] Distinguish between common insolvency terms.

- [ ] State the general priority of creditors in an insolvency.

- [ ] List those creditors who are treated preferentially.

- [ ] Outline the rules relating to set off.

- [ ] Outline the law relating to antecedent transactions.

- [ ] Discuss the difference between bankruptcy and rescue of individuals.

In this text we have mentioned insolvency on a number of occasions – when opening an account, when being notified of a bankruptcy and when lending and taking security. This chapter covers some key aspects of insolvency as it relates to individuals and companies and introduces some additional practical implications for bankers.

Insolvency law has ancient origins and through the ages creditors, owed money that is not repaid, have sought to punish debtors. In 1761 the UK saw its last hanging for a bankruptcy offence. During the 19th Century debtor's gaols were used to imprison debtors. In the 1883 Bankruptcy Act, however, the reformer Joseph Chamberlain laid down rules that governed practice for 100 years. These rules allowed debtors to sell their assets in order to repay creditors and then to be discharged from their debts. These rules were later adopted into Company Law and in 1986, in a new Insolvency Act, they were updated and amalgamated under one statute. The 1986 Act also introduced insolvency regimes that would allow rehabilitation of debtors without bankruptcy occurring.

Since 1986, therefore, the choice has been between selling assets to repay creditors and rehabilitation or rescue. On the corporate side creditors have ensured that few rescues occur. On the individual side, however, nearly all insolvencies, where assets are present, are dealt with as rescues. Figure 16 summarizes the various insolvency regimes available:

Figure 16
Insolvency regimes

	Non-rescue	*Rescue*
Individual	Bankruptcy	Individual Voluntary Arrangement (IVA)
Corporate	Liquidation	Administration Corporate Voluntary Arrangement (CVA) Administrative Receivership

For bankers the important thing to remember is that Liquidation or bankruptcy ends the banker/customer relationship whereas use of a rescue regime may not. Indeed the bank may be asked to lend new money to allow a rescue to take place.

Insolvency-a definition

Although the word 'insolvent' has no one legal definition, it is generally understood to refer to one (or both) of the following situations:

(i) The debtor is unable to pay debts as they fall due for payment (for example, because of a short-term cash-flow problem). As a result bankers are amont the first to detect signs of insolvency in customers.

(ii) Looking at a balance sheet for the debtor, the debtor's liabilities exceed the value of assets, taking account of the costs of realizing the assets.

You should note however that these two 'tests' of insolvency are not necessarily the basis on which the courts decide, for example, whether or not a company should be wound up. A company may be put into liquidation even though it is solvent (for example, where the number of shareholders in a company falls below the minimum of two).

Insolvency regimes

Insolvency numbers are strongly linked to the state of the economy and so in a recession it would be expected that insolvencies would rise. In 2000 company insolvencies were enjoying a decreasing trend with 14,317 liquidations and 2,590 company rescues. Individual insolvency, however, was increasing with 22,042 bankruptcies and 8,204 IVAs. This was largely associated with the huge increases in consumer credit. Year 2001 figures indicate increases in all of these figures – a possible sign of impending recession and potential problems and losses for banks and other lenders.

Bankruptcy

This is where an insolvent individual is petitioned in court by a creditor owed over £750 and left unpaid for three weeks. Debtors may also make themselves bankrupt. Once the court makes a Bankruptcy Order the bankrupt loses legal title to any assets that may be owned (except for those assets needed to sustain basic comforts or to continue to earn an income – cars, tools of the trade and personal clothing are often excluded in this way). The title to assets now vests in the Trustee in Bankruptcy, a licensed practitioner, or the Official Receiver who then proceeds to sell the assets and distribute funds to the creditors.

Most bankruptcies are automatically discharged after three years but can be extended for repeated bankruptcy or where debtors do not cooperate with the Trustee.

Liquidation

Also known as 'Winding-Up', this is bankruptcy for companies and partnerships. In this case a Liquidator is appointed who has similar powers and duties to the Trustee. The difference between companies and individuals is that liquidations are not discharged; instead the company is dissolved once its business has either been sold or the assets sold off.

Rescues

Rescue regimes for individuals and companies in the UK are increasing in use. The main similarity of the Voluntary Arrangement and Administration schemes is that debtors can put forward a compromise or deal to their creditors and continue to trade and earn funds to pay off debts rather than simply closing them down. Rescues often result in better returns for creditors but are, by their nature, more uncertain of success.

For Individuals the key rescue regime is the IVA. An insolvent individual may apply to the court for protection while thrashing out a deal with creditors. There are no rules stipulating what the deal can be but creditors will want a better return than they would achieve in bankruptcy. In this way debtors, by being allowed to continue to trade or operate as professionals, such as Solicitors or Accountants, can earn money to pay off creditors. For a banker as creditor the decision is often whether to agree to the deal (75% of creditors must agree to make it binding) or to reject it and opt for bankruptcy. The hope of helping and retaining a customer will be a factor in the bank's thinking as well as the potential repayment. For a debtor the IVA provides a way to retain assets otherwise available to a Trustee in Bankruptcy and to replace these with income contributions or assets from other people (perhaps family members).

Lastly, in this section, we need to mention Administrative Receivership. This is a remedy for a floating charge holder (normally a bank) but may be abolished in the Enterprise Act 2002, which is currently going through Parliament. Administrative Receivership has been important to banks in the past and its abolition may well change lending policy (see later where floating charge holders appear in the priority of creditors).

The priority of creditors

In any insolvency the creditors must be paid in a pre-determined order. Some creditors enjoy higher priority than others because of the type of debt they hold. The full order of priority is as follows:

a) Secured creditors. Holders of fixed-charge security enjoy their own legal remedies and do not, officially, take part in the insolvency unless their security is insufficient to cover their debt.

b) Expenses of the insolvency. This includes the costs of the petitioning creditor, the official receiver and the trustee in bankruptcy or liquidator.

c) Preferential debts. Those creditors such as the Inland Revenue, VAT or wages, having preferred status under Schedule 6 IA.

d) Floating charges (where applicable, in corporate insolvency only). While the floating charge is a type of security, the holder's rights to business assets is subject to the duty to pay preferential creditors in full.

e) Ordinary debts. These form the vast majority of debts in an insolvency. Ordinary trade creditors fare rather badly in terms of creditor priority but often possess information that can reveal additional assets that can then be realized for the benefit of all creditors.

f)   Interest on preferential and ordinary debts.

g)   Deferred debts plus interest thereon. These are debts owed to 'associates' of the insolvent (such as family members) or 'connected persons' of the insolvent company (such as directors). By giving these debts the lowest priority outside creditors have a better chance of recovery.

Secured creditors

Secured creditors are creditors who have a fixed charge on a particular part of the debtor's assets. For example, a building society will have a fixed charge on the creditor's mortgaged house. Secured creditors cannot 'prove' (that is provide evidence) for their debts in an insolvency (except by waiving their right to the security) because they can realize their security to pay the debt (for example, the building society could sell the house to repay the mortgage). If the security realizes less than the full amount of the debt, a secured creditor has the following options:

- Prove for the unsecured balance as an ordinary creditor;

- 'Value' the security and prove for the balance;

- Surrender their security and prove as unsecured for their whole debt. This is important in 'rescue' situations because, for example, it may be vital for the debtor to retain the business premises so that trading can continue.

The class of secured creditors also includes:

- Creditors with hire purchase contracts, where ownership of the financed asset is retained by the lender until the debt is fully paid;

- Creditors with supply contracts containing retention of title clauses, as long as they can identify the actual goods supplied;

- Creditors with guarantees from third parties that cover the debt are not classed as secured. They can pursue their remedies against the guarantor and, separately, against the insolvent debtor by proving in the bankruptcy or liquidation.

Preferential creditors

The law gives priority to certain debtors (known as 'preferential creditors') over the bankrupt's ordinary creditors. They are paid in proportion to the size of their respective debt where there is insufficient money in the estate to pay all of the preferential creditors in full. Where this situation arises, the ordinary and deferred creditors will of course receive no dividend at all. Preferential debts of the insolvent debtor shall be paid in priority to other debts.

Preferential creditors are listed in section 386 IA and more fully in Schedule 6 of the Act. They consist of:

- debts due to the Inland Revenue (unpaid PAYE for the 12 months prior to the bankruptcy or winding-up order only). This specifically excludes income tax due on the previous year's income or profits.

- debts due to Customs and Excise. This principally covers unpaid VAT for the six-month period prior to the bankruptcy or winding-up order. Also included are road fund tax (12-months) and betting and bingo duties (12 months).

- social security contributions. (All unpaid class 1 and/or class 2 contributions for the 12 month period prior to bankruptcy or winding-up.)

- contributions payable to occupational pension schemes by a bankrupt.

- remuneration of employees employed by the insolvent debtor prior to the bankruptcy or winding-up to cover:

- unpaid wages (up to four months before the bankruptcy order but only to the extent of £800 per employee);

- holiday pay and redundancy pay up to a specific maximum figure.

Money borrowed by the debtor to pay wages (subject to the above limits) is treated as a preferential debt. As a result banks can often claim part of their debt as preferential by identifying the advances they have made for wages as separate from the other advances they have made to the borrower.

Government proposals in July 2001 suggested a readiness to give up 'Crown preference', leaving only wages as preferential – which would mean more funds for ordinary creditors in most insolvencies.

Ordinary debts

Here the vast bulk of trade creditors and unsecured lenders lie. In most cases they are unlikely to receive much return on their loan at all. If Crown Preference and Floating Charges are abolished the ordinary creditors may benefit. However, the likelihood is that banks will seek other security or provide alternative finance such as factoring of debts and leasing of assets in order to avoid losses.

Principles of priority

- Pari-passu

- Cascade

- Set Off

The Latin phrase *pari passu* indicates that creditors are paid equally within their creditor class (priority level) or equally in proportion to their debts if there are insufficient assets to meet all the debts in that particular class.

The Cascade principle means that ordinary creditors receive nothing until after preferential debts have been satisfied in full.

Although many insolvencies fail even to cover the fees of the insolvency practitioner or official receiver, a common scenario is for preferential creditors to be paid in full and for ordinary creditors to be paid pro rata (so many pence in the pound).

Set off relates to mutual debts, mutual credits and mutual dealings between creditors and debtors. Set off must be implemented before the debt is proved (that is claimed from the insolvent estate). Set off rules are covered in Chapter 8.

Case study

Colin Beech, a retail florist, has been a customer of your bank for a number of years. He currently owes your bank £10,000 on overdraft but you have been advised today that he has had a bankruptcy order made against him on a petition from the Inland Revenue. Colin's statement of affairs shows other creditors with claims on the assets available.

The estimated values of Colin's assets (after disposal costs) are as follows:

Asset	Estimated value (£)
Assets available to trustee	10,000
House	80,000

Colin's marital home is owned jointly by Colin and his wife and has a mortgage from a building society of £60,000 outstanding.

Other creditors (including your claim) are as follows:

Creditor	Value of claim (£)
Bank overdraft (unsecured)	10,000
24 months unpaid PAYE	6,000
Ordinary trade creditors	15,000
Three weeks' wages for three staff	1,000

In addition the trustee estimates the expenses of the bankruptcy to total £5,000.

In this example, the equity from the marital home will be split between Colin and his wife (50% as default). The proceeds may take some time to materialize.

Assets available	£	£
Available assets	10,000	
50% of house equity	10,000	
Total assets available		20,000
Creditors		
Trustees Fees	5,000	
	leaves	15,000
Preferential Creditors		
12 months unpaid PAYE	3,000	
Three weeks wages for three staff	1,000	
Total preferentials (paid in full)	4,000	
	leaves	11,000
Bank overdraft	10,000	
Ordinary trade creditors	15,000	
12 months unpaid PAYE	3,000	
Total unsecureds	28,000	
	div.	£11,000 divided by £28,000
		39.3p in £

Thus your bank should receive £10,000 x 39.3% = £3,930. A loss of £6,070 will ultimately be used to reduce bank profits. The bank could have protected itself by taking security of a second mortgage over the house, subject to the building society charge.

Antecedent transactions

Transactions entered into by the insolvent debtor before the bankruptcy or winding-up order can have the effect of considerably reducing the value of the assets available to creditors. Past practice has been to 'sell' assets to a relative or to an associated company for a reduced value, or to prefer certain creditors, repaying them rather than the body of creditors. Where such practice is evident today the transactions can be reversed by application to the court. Reversal of transactions can increase the value of the estate and of the dividend available to creditors. The main types of antecedent transactions are:

- transactions at an undervalue

- preferences

Transactions at an undervalue
These are transactions entered into by the debtor:

- within 'a relevant time' before the onset of insolvency, and

- at an undervalue, that is for less than its full value at the time of the transaction.

The law relating to transactions at an undervalue is similar for both individuals and companies but the Insolvency Act (IA) sections and relevant time limits are different in each case. The time limit for undervalues is 2 years for an individual and 5 for a company. For preferences the time limit for both is 6 months – unless an associate has been preferred when the limit rises to 2 years.

An example of an undervalue in bankruptcy was seen in *Re Kumar* (1993) where a £140,000 house was transferred to the spouse in return for her assuming responsibility for the £30,000 mortgage.

In corporate insolvency a good example was seen in *Aveling Barford Ltd v Perion Ltd* and others (1989). The transfer of a property at an undervalue to a company controlled by the principal shareholder of the insolvent company was reversed upon application by an administrative receiver. Normally a liquidator has the power to challenge preferences and transactions at an undervalue, but cannot reverse them. In this case, the transfer was ultra vires (beyond the power) of the shareholder and, therefore, could be reversed.

However, in *Re M C Bacon Ltd* (1990) it was held that the giving of a debenture to a bank to secure existing and future borrowing was not a transaction at an undervalue.

Where a liquidator, working on behalf of creditors, finds that an undervalue transaction has taken place within the specified time limit the court can be approached for the transaction to be reversed. Although this is not always possible it does mean that a bank may find more assets available to it as a creditor where assets are added back into the debtor's estate.

Preferences

Preferences are transactions where a creditor of the debtor has been paid in preference to other creditors prior to the issuing of a bankruptcy or winding-up petition. For example a debtor, knowing he is insolvent, pays a significant sum to a relative to whom he owes that sum. The calculated effect of this payment is therefore to allow one creditor to benefit at the expense of the others.

The Insolvency Act 1986 allows the court to make orders in similar terms to those in transactions at an undervalue providing that:

a)   prior to the issue of the petition, the debtor has done something which has the effect of putting a creditor or surety or guarantor in a better position than they would otherwise be in if bankruptcy or winding up occurs;

b)   in giving the preference, the debtor was influenced by a desire to put the creditor, guarantor or surety in such a better position. The insolvency test also applies;

c)   the preference was given within the relevant time limit.

Banks, therefore, need to be aware of preferences because money received from a debtor could subsequently be reclaimed by a trustee or liquidator if it was received within six months prior to the issue of a bankruptcy or winding-up petition. In practice, where pressure has been brought to bear on the debtor by the bank, and the debtor has no motive to prefer that creditor (other than the fear of court proceedings or execution) the court is unlikely to make an order for the return of the money to the estate.

A possible scenario that would disadvantage a bank would be where the debtor has paid a large sum into a bank account from sales without paying suppliers and, therefore, reduced the overdraft substantially. It then transpires that the bank holds a guarantee or mortgage from the debtor's spouse or the company's directors as security for the overdraft. On such facts, it is not difficult to infer the appropriate motive on the debtor's part. The bank may then be obliged to repay the appropriate sum for the benefit of the creditors as a whole.

Summary

In this chapter you have learned that:

- creditor priority rules and rules relating to certain antecedent transactions for individuals are similar to those for companies

- preferential creditors have priority over ordinary creditors but have limits to the extent of their claims

- all creditors rank equally, pro rata, within their own class of creditor

- certain antecedent transactions can be reopened in insolvency for the general benefit of creditors

- Mutual credits, debits and dealings can be set off between the debtor and the creditor before proving in the insolvency.

Further Reading

Eales P, (1996), *Insolvency: A practical legal handbook for managers*, Gresham Books.
   http://www.insolvency.co.uk
   http://www.insolvency.gov.uk

Glossary

Assets
Tangible or intangible possessions such as buildings (tangible) or bank loans (intangible assets of bankers).

APACS
Association of Payment Clearing Services; it runs the credit and debit clearings in the UK.

ATM
Automated Teller Machine (Cash dispenser).

BACS
Formerly known as Bankers Automated Clearing Services, this is a system for businesses to make credit transfers to bank accounts of their employees or suppliers.

Bailment
A contract whereby a person (the bailor) lodges goods for repair or safe custody with a repairer or bank (the bailee).

Bank of England
The UK's Central bank, the government's bank and the 'lender of last resort' to commercial banks.

Banking
This is what banks do. It entails deposit and lending services and money transmission.

Banking Code
A voluntary code of conduct subscribed to by banks and building societies outlining the banker / customer contract and the rights and duties of banks and building societies and their customers.

Bankruptcy
A legal remedy whereby a debtors assets are sold and the proceeds distributed amongst his/her creditors.

Barter
Direct exchange of goods for goods, without the need for money.

Bill of Exchange
An unconditional order in writing, drawn by a creditor on a debtor, requiring the payment of a stated sum of money on demand or on a fixed date in the future.
(See Section 3 Bills of Exchange Act 1882).

BBA
British Bankers' Association.

Broad Money
The total of money in a country used to make payments and as a store of value. This includes notes, coin, and current and savings accounts.

BSA
Building Societies Association.

Capital
The liability of a business to its owners. The excess of a firm's assets over its liabilities.

CBT
Collecting Bank Truncation.

CD
Certificate of Deposit, usually of £50,000 or more.

CP
Commercial Paper.

CHAPS
Clearing House Automated Payments System, for high value immediate payments.

Cheque
A Bill of Exchange drawn on a banker and payable on demand. (See Section 73 Bills of Exchange Act 1882).

City of London
The location of many traders in financial and commodity markets. Once limited to the 'Square Mile' the 'City' now has participants in 'Docklands' areas.

Conversion
A legal tort (a wrong) whereby rightful owners are denied their goods. In relation to cheques this means the payment of a cheque to somebody other than the rightful owner.

Credit Card
A plastic card issued by a bank or credit card company enabling the holder to purchase goods on a credit basis.

Credit Scoring
A statistical method of measuring risks in a personal lending situation by reference to the loan application from answers provided by a prospective borrower.

Current Account
An account with a bank or building society on which cheques may be drawn.

DD
Direct Debit. (Used only by creditors sponsored by their banks to directly debit their debtors' bank accounts on a regular basis. Used for mortgage repayments, insurance premiums, council tax, etc).

Debit Card
A plastic card issued by a bank or building society enabling the holder to purchase goods and to immediately debit their account at the issuing bank or building society. Many cards are multi-function and can also be used as a cheque guarantee card or to draw cash from an ATM.

Deposit Account
A bank deposit account is a savings account, normally demanding 7 days notice for withdrawals. In a building society the deposit account holder enjoys greater priority over other investors should the society get into difficulties and the account usually attracts a lower interest rate.

Derivatives
Transactions giving the right to buy or sell a security at some time in the future.

EFTPOS
Electronic Funds Transfer at Point of Sale.

EMU
Economic and Monetary Union.

Equitable Mortgage
Created by deposit of title deeds with the intention that they are treated as security. Weaker than a full legal mortgage, the security provider also agrees to create a legal mortgage should the bank call upon him/her to do so.

Equity
This has three relevant meanings:
- The difference between the value of a property and the loan outstanding on it (can be negative);
- Ordinary Shares;
- An ancient system of law derived from the decisions of courts.

ERM
Exchange Rate Mechanism.

Euro
The new currency of 11 of the member states of the European Union with effect from 4 January 1999. Notes and coins were introduced in 2002.

Exchange Rate
The price of one country's money in terms of another country's money.

Financial Intermediary
An organization or person (salesperson) who intermediates between ultimate lenders and ultimate borrowers.

Financial Ombudsman Service
This statutory body resolves disputes between customers and banks and other financial institutions, where complaints against the institution are deadlocked.

Fiscal Policy
A government policy tool concerned with the revenue from taxes and government expenditure and borrowing.

Foreign Exchange
A generic term meaning other countries' currencies.

FSA
Financial Services Authority, also Financial Services Act 1986.

Gilts
'Gilt edged' securities or low risk securities issued by the UK government.

Giro
A centralised payments system, used widely in Europe, in which debtors use full bank account details of their creditors to effect payments.

Guarantee
A written agreement for one person (the Guarantor) to be liable for the debt or default of another.

IBDE
Inter-Bank Data Exchange, an agreed system and procedure linking all participating banks for the rapid electronic transmission of data.

IHCF
Industry Hot Card File, a list of stolen credit and debit cards made available to retailers.

ISA
Individual Savings Account.

Inflation
The phenomenon of rising prices (falling purchasing power of money.) (See also RPI and RPIX.)

Insolvency
Where assets exceed liabilities or due debts cannot be paid.

Interest
The price of borrowed money. Credit interest is paid by banks which 'borrow' funds from depositors, while customers who borrow from banks pay debit interest.

Investment Banks
Wholesale Banks (q.v.) which concentrate on buying and selling securities and derivatives rather than lending and borrowing money.

Laundering
The transmission of cash via the banking system with the objective of hiding or masking its origin. Normally associated with criminal activity.

Law
A system of dispute settlement between society and individuals (criminal law) and between individuals (civil law). English law is derived from the outcomes of court cases and from custom (common law) and Acts of Parliament (statute law).

Legal Charge / Mortgage
A contract between a lender and a borrower (or security provider) giving the lender rights (including sale) over an asset following the default of the borrower.

Liabilities
Debts owed by one person or organisation to another. Bank liabilities include funds deposited in accounts by customers.

LIFFE
London International Financial Futures and Options Exchange, the UK's major derivatives market.

Loan
The borrowing of a sum of money, usually for an agreed period and at an agreed rate of interest. Loans can be repaid on a monthly basis, annually or at the end of the loan period (bullet repayment).

Merchant Banks
Wholesale Banks (q.v.) which specialise in financing trade. Many have become investment banks.

MFI
Monetary Financial Institution: A European Union term for bank or building society.

Monetary Policy
Government manipulation of the macroeconomy with specific reference to the quantity of money in circulation and the prevailing interest rate.

Money

Any asset acceptable by society as a medium of exchange, a store of value and a unit of account. Notes and coins in circulation are most obviously money but so too are credit balances in bank accounts and credit available to borrowers.

Money Markets

Markets where money is bought and sold. These comprise the Discount Market, the CD market and the CP market among others.

Mortgage

Colloquially, a loan to buy a house but in legal terms a mortgage gives a lender legal rights over an asset should the loan not be repaid.

Mortgage Code

A voluntary code outlining the rights and duties of mortgage lenders and borrowers (see also Banking Code).

MT

Mail Transfer (of funds).

Narrow Money

The total of money used in a country as a means of payment. Normally includes only notes and coins but sometimes includes current accounts.

NBFI

Non-Bank Financial Intermediary.

Negotiable Instrument

Any instrument that can be used to pass title by delivery of the instrument. Bills of Exchange (q.v.) are negotiable, as were cheques before 1992 when the words 'Account Payee' rendered them non-negotiable.

NMS

Normal Market Size.

OFI
Other Financial Intermediary: A European Union term for Insurance Company or Pension Fund.

OTC
Over-the-Counter market.

Overdraft
An agreed credit limit set on a running current account, allowing the borrower to use and re-use the credit facility until the overdraft period expires.

PEP
Personal Equity Plan

PIN
Personal Identification Number

Principal
The original (capital) amount of a loan, later reduced by repayment of capital or increased by non-payment of interest. The term also describes a person giving instructions to an agent such as customers giving instructions to their bank to buy or sell shares.

Reference
Also known as a status enquiry. References are used by creditors as part of their credit assessment procedures and are requests for a banker or trader to give an opinion on the financial stability of the bank customer in respect of a particular transaction.

Regulated Agreement
A personal lending agreement for less than £25,000 regulated by the Consumer Credit Act 1974.

Retail Banks
Banks accepting business from personal and small business customers through a network of local branches or postal- or telephone-based accounts.

Risk
The statistical chance of a negative event such as fire, death or theft. In business this is the chance of a deal not being completed, a loan not being repaid or other event such as computer breakdown.

RPI
Retail Prices Index, sometimes called 'headline inflation'.

RPIX
Retail Prices index excluding interest paid on mortgages, also called 'underlying inflation'.

S/O
Standing Order, a regular payment from a current account.

Safe Custody
The bailment (q.v.) service offered by some banks, whereby valuables are placed in a bank's vault for safekeeping.

Secrecy
One of the important duties owed by a banker to the customer. The duty of secrecy survives even the death of the account holder and the closure of the account. There are some legally acceptable exceptions to the general rule.

Security
Sometimes referred to as 'Collateral', security describes the assets provided under a legal charge or mortgage. Security ownership moves to the banker if the principal debt is not repaid.
The word 'Securities' also denotes financial instruments traded on a stock exchange such as company shares or Gilts (q.v.).

Set Off
A banker has the right to net or combine accounts held in the same name and same capacity, provided the sums in each account are certain (no contingent liabilities). This is important when the banker / customer relationship ends through the death, bankruptcy etc of the customer.

SFA
Securities and Futures Authority.

Smart Card
A plastic credit or debit card with the ability to store transaction information via an embedded silicon chip. Smart cards extend and enlarge the capabilities of the magnetic stripe cards used widely in the UK and USA. Smart Cards are used extensively in France.

SRO
Self Regulatory Organisation. Five SROs were set up under the Financial Services Act 1986 for providers of financial services to regulate their own activities. Mergers have reduced these to three: IMRO, PIA and SFA. All were be combined in the FSA by the year 2001.

SWIFT
Society for Worldwide Interbank Financial Telecommunication, an international messages system for making payments in different currencies.

TARGET
Trans European Automated Gross Settlement Express Transfer. An instantaneous payments system set up in January 1999 for the whole European Union.

Truncation
The curtailment of the cheque clearing process before the clearing cycle is complete. Truncation allows electronic transaction messages to supersede physical presentation of cheques.

TT
Telegraphic Transfer (of funds).

VADD
Variable Amount Direct Debit. A direct debit authority with no set amount. This enables originating users, such as mortgage lenders, to vary repayment levels without the debtor needing to take action.

Wholesale Banks

Banks which do not offer accounts through local branches or postal or telephone facilities. Instead they concentrate on transactions for large amounts of money from a selected range of companies or from other banks.

Index

Ability	211	Banker, the paying	199
Acceptability	25	Banker's drafts	157, 169
Accountancy	4	Banker-customer relationship	108
Accounts, business and other	135	Banking code	98, 120
closing	129	Banking system, the	34
joint	132	changes in	8
opening	126	private	79
Advances	76	Banking, the business of	10
Agency	131	Bankruptcy	130, 243
APACS	177	Banks	32
operational groupings	183	other activities of	77
Appropriation	144	retail	79
Assets	73	wholesale	80
other	77	Banks' assets, controlling the	43
ATM cards	156	Bills	75
		Bills of exchange	173
BACS Ltd	180	Building societies	61, 83
Bailor and bailee	110	Building society cheques	158
Balances at the Bank of England	74		
Bank, what is a?	106	Capital	73
Bank accounts, managing	142	Card payments group	183
Bank charge forms – key clauses	226	Case studies	215, 249
Bank decision	216, 218	Case 1: Bill Adams – bridging loan	215
Bank giro credits (credit transfers)	161		
Bank of England	63, 99	Case 2: Cliff Ramsbotham – overdraft	216
Bank's duties to its customers	111		
duty of care when giving advice	116	Cash	150
		Cash services group	183
duty of secrecy	113	Certificates of deposits (CDs)	73

CHAPS Clearing Co Ltd   178, 179
Character   210
Charge cards   167
Cheque and Credit Clearing Co Ltd   178
Cheque card fraud and misuse   154
Cheque guarantee cards   152
Cheques   151
    a sum certain in money   173
    account payee   196
    alterations   197
    an unconditional order   172
    elsewhere   202
    endorsement   194
    examining the cheque: the
    paying banker   201
    general and special crossings   196
    house   200
    in writing and signed   172
    not mutilated   197
    not negotiable   197
    other risks   205
    payee's name   193
    returning   206
    signature   197
    special presentations   200
    stops   203
    suspicious circumstances   198
    the amount   193
    the back of the cheque   202
    the collecting bank: examining
    cheques   192
    the crossing   195
    the date on the cheque   193
    the front of the cheque   201
    through the cheque clearing   200
    to a banker   172
    to or to the order of a specified
    person, or to bearer   173
    to pay on demand or at a fixed or
    determinable future date   172

    types of endorsement   194
    what is cheque truncation?   185
    what is a cheque?   171
    when is an endorsement required?   194
City markets group and corporate
    payments   183
Clayton's case   142
Cleared and uncleared funds   207
Clearings, the traditional   175
Clubs and associations   140
Combination or set off   145
Commercial banks   70
Commission   214
Communication, changes in   7
Companies   136
Company bank account, opening a   139
Company documents   137
Conclusive evidence   228
Consideration   227
Consumer protection   97
Continuing security   227
Contract, when is a contract not a
    contract?   224
Credit cards   162
Credit scoring   219
Creditors, preferential   247
    secured   246
    the priority of   245
Customer, who is a?   107
Customer's duties to the bank   117
Customer's life, events occurring
    during the   129

Death   130
Debit cards   155
Debtor and creditor   108
Demand   227
Deposits   72
Direct debits   159
DIVAN   237

Divisibility	24
Divorce	133
Durability	25
Duress and undue influence	225
Duties and rights, additional	119
Economics	5
Equities	92
Estate agencies and insurance companies	78
Euro, the	166
European Union monetary policy	44
Exchange rates and interest rates	40
Executor and trustee business	79
Executors and administrators	140
Extras	214
Fiduciary element, A special or	110
Financial intermediation	94
Financial regulation	95
Financial stability	100
Fiscal policy	45
Fixed exchange rates	43
Foreign banks	63
Foreign currency	168
Foreign exchange dealing	77
Further Reading	11, 30, 49
	67, 88, 103
	123, 147, 170, 189
	208, 221, 253, 239
Gilts	91
Girobank Plc	81
Global custody	78
Government	35
Government borrowing and debt repayment	36
Guarantees	236

History of banking and finance,	
1694-1950	51
1951-1970	53
1971-1985	55
1986 to date	56
ICE	214
IMRO	96
Increase in value	234
Individual Voluntary Arrangement (IVA)	242
Index-linking	40
Inflation and deflation	37
Inflation target	44
Inflation, causes of	38
links with	41
measuring	38
Insolvency, a definition	243
regimes	243
Insurance	85
Insurance (Security)	213
Interest	214
Interest rates	43
Investments	76
Jack committee	119
Joint and several liability	227
Land	229, 232, 234, 235
Law	4
changes in the	7
Legal mortgage	231
Lending	5
Lending, principles of	210
Life assurance polices	230, 233, 234, 236
Liquid assets	77
Liquidation	244
Liquidity	26

Lloyd's   94
London International Financial
    Futures and Options
    Exchange (LIFFE)   93
London Stock Exchange   90

M0   28
M4   29
Market loans   74
Markets, other   93
Marketability   233
Marketing   6
Marriage or change of name   131
Married women   133
Means/margin   211
Mental incapacity   129
Minors   134
Misrepresentation   225
Mistake   224
Monetary policy   42
Monetary policy, forms of   43
Monetary stability   99
Money   3
    a liquid store of value   19
    a medium of exchange   19
    a standard of deferred payments   21
    a unit of account   21
    a world without   13
    changes in   7
    characteristics of   22
    functions of   18
    how it is created   32
    in England and Wales,
    a brief history of   15
    is an asset   26
    liquidity and assets used as
    money   26
    measuring the stock or supply of   28
    today   27
    value of   37

Money supply targets (later
    monitoring ranges)   43
Mortgagor/mortgagee   110

National savings bank   82
Negotiability   186
Negotiable instruments   185
Notes and coins   74

Operations in financial markets   101
Ordinary debts   248
Overseas residents   36

Pari-passu   248
Partnerships   136
Payment, international means of   168
People   3
Personal covenant to repay   228
Personal customers   126
Personal Investment Authority   96
Pitfalls, avoiding the   226
Point of sale, procedure at the   153
Portability   23
Preferences   252
Principal and agent   109
Printing   102
Priority, principles of   248
Professionals, other   140
Protection funds   97
Public and private companies   138
Purpose   211

Recognizability   24
Repayment and term   212
Rescues   244

Saving   45
    emergencies   46
    for an increase in wealth   46

for old age   46
for the family   46
future expenditure   45
how people save   47
reasons why people save   45
to establish a track record   46
to fulfil a contract   47
tradition   46
Security   223
    testing for good   228
Security-taking procedures   237
Service of demand   228
SFA   96
Share registration   78
Sight deposits   72
Smart cards   165
Sole traders   135
Solicitors   139
Spreading the risks   34
Stability and scarcity   23
Standing orders   158
Statutory protection for the
    collecting banker   198

Stocks and shares   230, 233, 234, 235
Store cards   167

Taxation and spending   35
Technology   6
Telegraphic and mail transfers   169
Time deposits   73
Time limits for decisions   200
Town clearing   179
Transactions at an undervalue   251
Transactions, antecedent   251
Traveller's cheques   168
Truncation   184
Trustees   141

Uniformity   23

Valuation   229

Whole debt clause   226